french on display

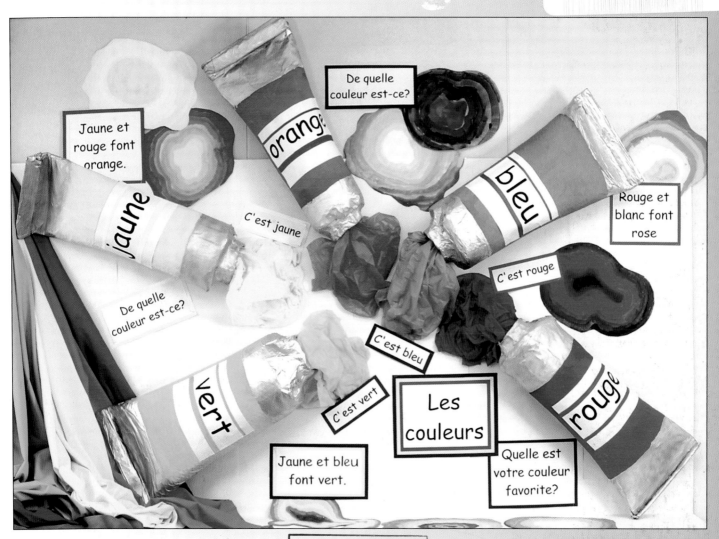

Hilary Ansell

Acknowledgements

I would like to thank all of the children from the following schools whose work has been photographed for this book. I have enjoyed working with you all.

Town Field Primary School
Kingfisher Primary School
Hexthorpe Primary School
Mallard Primary School
Warmsworth Primary School
Barnburgh Primary School
Woodlands Primary School

A very big thank you to the staff of those schools which have supported me. A special thank you to Lynn Hughes at Town Field Primary for working on her own to produce some superb displays. A special thank you also to Jane Squires. Your enthusiasm is inspirational and your displays are wonderful!

Thank you once again to all of my friends at St John's Hospice, Doncaster, for your unfailing support and interest in all that I do.

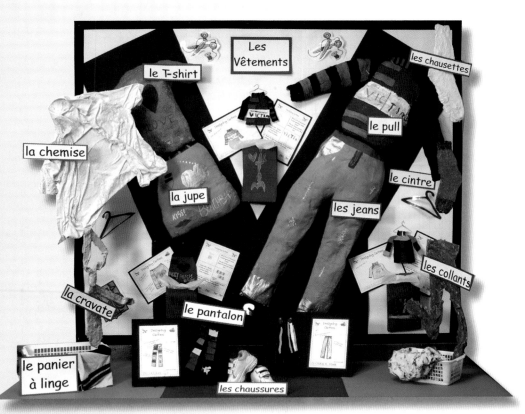

Clothes (Les Vêtements) (page 16)

First published in 2006 by Belair Publications.

Apex Business Centre, Boscombe Road, Dunstable, LU5 4RL.
Email: belair@folens.com

Commissioning editor: Zoë Nichols   Editor: Jennifer Steele
Page Layout: Suzanne Ward   Photography: RB Photography   Cover Design: Steve West

© 2006 Folens on behalf of the author.

British Library Cataloguing in Publication Data. A catalogue record for this publication is available from the British Library.

ISBN 0 94788 446 0

Contents

Introduction

The aims of teaching a modern foreign language are to develop linguistic skills and to increase awareness of other countries, their peoples and their customs. Children are more receptive towards learning a foreign language when they are younger. If time and resources allow, it is an excellent idea to introduce a modern foreign language early, starting with simple greetings and answering the register. The use of action songs, rhymes, puppets and very simple well-illustrated stories makes the learning process fun. When learning is fun, it happens naturally.

Je me réveille.

Je me lève.

Je me lave.

Je prends le petit déjeuner.

Je m'habille.

Je me brosse les dents.

Je prends l'autobus

J'arrive à l'école.

Il est six heures.

Quelle heure est-il?

Quelle heure est-il?

Il est deux heures moins dix.

Quelle heure est-il?

Il est dix heures dix.

Quelle heure est-il?

Il est onze heures cinq.

Teaching and Learning French

With older children, work can advance through direct teaching in whole-class and small group situations.

The themes in this book are divided into the following sections:

- **Starting Points** In this section, suggestions are given for introducing the theme. Whole-class games practise the basic vocabulary.

- **Further Activities** Here, ideas for practising the key vocabulary are given, usually linked to an art and design activity.

- **Conversation Model** This useful section gives a very basic outline for practice with the children.

- **Making the Display** Instructions for creating a colourful and interactive display are given, linked to the theme.

- **Vocabulary** This useful box lists some basic vocabulary to refer to when teaching the theme.

Learning another language presents opportunities for the reinforcement of knowledge developed in other areas of the curriculum. Many of the activities outlined in *French on Display* are cross-curricular. Aspects of History, Geography, Mathematics, RE, Art, PE and ICT are all included. The book presents French vocabulary, conversation models and simple grammar in 33 well-illustrated themes that may be adapted for use at a number of levels, from the simple presentation of key vocabulary to more advanced question and answer situations. The aim is to enable children to feel confident enough to express themselves in a foreign language without feeling self-conscious. It is more important that the children are happy to 'have a go' without embarrassment than to worry about getting everything grammatically correct.

Je vais à l'école.

Ideally, the learning of a modern foreign language should not be limited to fixed teaching sessions, but should occur naturally throughout the day. This, however, depends very much upon the resources of the school. It only remains to suggest that you dip into this book for ideas on how to introduce various topics, and that you adapt the suggestions for games and activities and have fun making the displays. Do not try to work through the book from cover to cover. It is an adaptable resource. Have fun with your French!

Hilary Ansell

Getting to Know You (On se Présente)

Starting Points

- Introduce yourself to the class. 'Je m'appelle Madame/Monsieur/Mademoiselle Smith.' (I am called Mrs/Mr/Miss Smith.)

- Call the register in French, addressing each child personally, 'Bonjour, Kate.' The child replies, 'Bonjour, Madame/Monsieur/Mademoiselle Smith.' Ask the children, 'Comment t'appelles-tu?' (What are you called?), to which they reply 'Je m'appelle …' (I am called …) Practise asking each other's names.

- Play the game 'Quelqu'un frappe à la porte. Qui est-ce?' (Someone's knocking on the door. Who is it?) Send two or three children out of the room. One child knocks on the door. Ask the class who it is: 'Qui est-ce?' A child replies, 'C'est Thomas.' and the child outside the door replies 'Oui, je m'appelle Thomas' or 'Non, ce n'est pas Thomas. Je m'appelle …'

Further Activities

- Draw left- and right-facing silhouettes of each other on black paper, cut out and mount these on contrasting paper. Use these to pose the question 'Qui est-ce?' in order to elicit the response, for example, 'C'est Kate.'

- Paint A3 portraits of each other. Use for the same purpose as above.

- Make fabric collaged portraits of each other using a variety of fabrics and wool. Ask 'Comment s'appelle-t-il/elle?' (What is he/she called?)

- Take photographs of the children using a digital camera. Print these out and mount on card with the caption 'Qui est-ce?'. Use the cards in a group game, asking the children to respond when you hold up a card 'C'est Thomas.', for example. Practise the negative form by holding up a card and deliberately saying the wrong name, for example 'C'est Sam?', to which a child replies 'Non, ce n'est pas Sam, c'est Paul.' (No, it's not Sam, it's Paul.)

Conversation Model

- 'Bonjour. Comment ça va?' (Hello. How are you?)
- 'Très bien, merci, et toi?' (Very well, thank you, and you?)
- 'Ça va bien.' (I'm well.)
- 'Comment t'appelles-tu?' (What are you called?)
- 'Je m'appelle Susanne. Comment t'appelles-tu?' (I'm called Susanne. What are you called?)
- 'Je m'appelle Paul. Au revoir, Susanne.' (I'm called Paul. Goodbye, Susanne.)
- 'Au revoir, Paul.' (Goodbye, Paul.)

Making the Display

- Mount the silhouettes and display so that they face each other. Add speech bubbles to the pairs, saying 'Comment ça va?' and 'Bien, merci' or 'Comment t'appelles-tu?' and 'Je m'appelle …'

- Cut out some of the painted portraits and mount as a group with the label 'Bonjour la classe!' and the reply in speech bubbles 'Bonjour, Madame/Monsieur…' Mount individual portraits with the child's name, for example, 'C'est Jade.'

- Trim and mount the fabric portraits and intersperse amongst the other artwork with relevant captions.

- Create a border of small silhouettes by folding strips of black paper and cutting out linked heads. Mount against a brightly coloured border strip.

Vocabulary

Bonjour, monsieur/madame/mademoiselle (Hello, sir/madam/miss)
Bonsoir (Good evening)
Bonne nuit (Goodnight)
Salut (Hello)
Au revoir (Goodbye)
Bonne journée (Have a good day.)
Comment ça va? (How are you?) Bien, merci. (Fine, thank you.)
Comment allez-vous? (How are you?) (child to adult) Pas mal, merci. (Not bad, thanks.)

The Family (La Famille)

Starting Points

- Ask the children about brothers and sisters. 'Tu as une soeur/un frère?' (Do you have a sister/brother?) The children respond 'Oui, j'ai un/deux/trois frère(s)' (Yes, I have one/two/three brother(s)) and so on, or 'Non. Je suis enfant unique.' (No. I'm an only child.)

- Ask the children to bring in photographs of members of their family. Introduce simple phrases to explain who they are. 'C'est mon père.' (This is my father.) 'C'est ma grand-mère.' (This is my grandmother.) and so on.

- Talk about occasions when families come together to celebrate. Ask the children to bring in photographs of family celebrations. Ask them to describe their relatives and compile a list of the adjectives they use. Give the French equivalent – grand(e) (tall), petite(e) (short), gros(se) (large), jolie (pretty), beau (handsome), belle (beautiful), mince (slim), timide (shy).

- Ask the children to describe the physical appearance of a family member. 'Il est grand.' (He is tall.) 'Il a les cheveux blonds.' (He has fair hair.) 'Il a les yeux bleus.' (He has blue eyes.)

Further Activities

- Cut out pictures from magazines and catalogues, mount on card and use these to practise describing people. 'Il est jeune.' (He is young.) 'Il est petit.' (He is little.) and so on.

- Draw, paint or collage pictures of family celebrations. The children say who the family members are. 'C'est ma tante.' (This is my aunt.) 'C'est ma cousine.' (This is my cousin.) and so on.

- Explain that for a display the children are going to make a picture of a wedding. Ask them to design the wedding outfits for the bride and groom and bridesmaids. Also make large fabric collages of wedding guests on stiff card.

- Design and make zigzag photograph albums for the children to give as presents to family members. Decorate the albums with braid and lace trim.

Making the Display

- Cut out the collaged figures and sort according to size. Staple the larger figures to the display board for the back row of the group.

- Attach small boxes/packets to the back of each figure in the next row to bring them forward slightly. Attach slightly larger boxes to the figures in the next row and so on to create a 3-D image.

- Add labels illustrating the vocabulary and a border of shiny paper to resemble a picture frame.

Conversation Model

- 'Tu as un frère, Daniel?' (Do you have a brother, Daniel?)

- 'Oui. J'ai un frère et une soeur.' (Yes. I've a brother and a sister.)

- 'Ton frère, quel âge a-t-il?' (How old is your brother?)

- 'Il a sept ans.' (He's seven.)

- 'Et ta soeur, quel age a-t-elle?' (And your sister, how old is she?)

- 'Elle a onze ans.' (She's eleven.)

- 'Ma soeur a treize ans.' (My sister's thirteen.)

Vocabulary

le bébé (baby)
le/la cousin(e) (cousin)
la fille unique (only daughter)
le fils unique (only son)
le frère (brother)
la grand-mère (grandmother)
le grand-père (grandfather)
la mère (mother)
le neveu (nephew)
la nièce (niece)
l'oncle (uncle)
le père (father)
la soeur (sister)
la tante (aunt)

Where Do You Live? (Où Habitez Vous?)

Starting Points

- Show the children a large-scale map or street plan of your area. Pose the question: 'Où habites-tu?/Où habitez-vous?' (Where do you live?)

- Make small marker flags using sticky labels and long pins for the children to mark where they live, saying as they do 'J'habite ici à Rue Stanley.' (I live in Stanley Road.)

- Locate your area on a map of the country and ask the children where they live. They reply 'J'habite à Warminster à l'Angleterre.' (I live in Warminster in England.) The children could then ask each other where they live.

Further Activities

- Ask each child to draw, paint or collage a picture of his/her house on card or stiff paper. Add a caption to the picture, such as 'J'habite dans une maison/un appartement/un pavillon/une maison mitoyenne.' (I live in a house/a flat/a bungalow/a semi-detached house.)

- Each child could draw/paint a picture of his/her front door with a clearly marked number. Use these to practise 'J'habite à numéro …' (I live at number …) Pose the question 'Où habite-il/elle?' (Where does he/she live?) The child in question holds up the door picture and another child answers 'Elle habite à numéro …' (She lives at number …)

- Using black crayon or pastel on grey or blue paper ask the children to draw twilight scenes of their streets. Highlight windows, street lamps and car headlights in yellow. Display with captions such as 'C'est ma rue.' (It's my street.) 'J'habite ici.' (I live here.)

- The children could make a clay tile of their house.

Conversation Model

- 'Où habites-tu, Jean?' (Where do you live, John?)

- 'J'habite à Doncaster.' (I live in Doncaster.)

- 'Où est Doncaster?' (Where's Doncaster?)

- 'Doncaster est dans le nord de l'Angleterre.' (Doncaster's in the north of England.)

- 'C'est une grande ville?' (Is it a big city?)

- 'Non. C'est une ville moyenne. Où habites-tu?' (No. It's a middle-sized town. Where do you live?)

- 'J'habite à Manchester. C'est une cité.' (I live in Manchester. It's a big city.)

Making the Display

- Make individual houses using collage and paint and position around the edges of the board to give the impression of a town/village.

- Add a large-scale street plan of your local area and a map of the British Isles.

- Use brightly coloured cord to join the houses to their position on the street plan. Mark the spot with a flag or map pin.

- Print out the key phrases and vocabulary. Mount on stiff card and add to the display.

- Paint and cut out A3-sized figures in profile as if they were walking down the street. Mount on stiff card and add speech bubbles using such phrases as 'Où habites-tu?'/'J'habite à numéro cinq.' Stand these in front of the display.

Vocabulary

L'Angleterre (England)
la campagne (the countryside)
le centre (the centre)
la cité (the city)
L'Ecosse (Scotland)
l'est (the east)
grand(e) (large)
L'Irlande (Ireland)
moyen(ne) (middle-sized)
le nord (the north)
l'ouest (the west)
Le Pays de Galles (Wales)
petit(e) (small)
le sud (the south)
le village (the village)
la ville (the town)

Sports and Hobbies (Les Sports et les Loisirs)

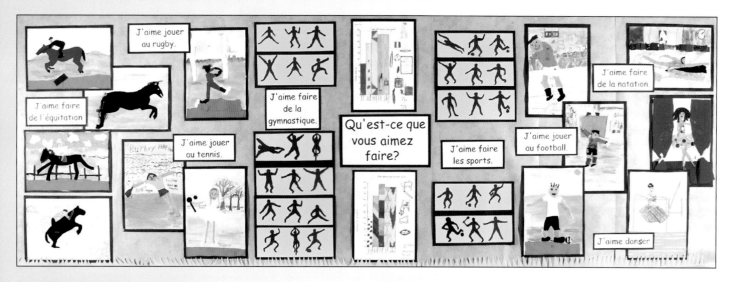

Starting Points

- Ask the children what they like to do in their free time. 'Qu'est-ce que vous aimez faire?' (What do you like to do?)

- Make a list of their favourite pastimes and practise saying them in French. 'J'aime regarder la television.' (I like to watch TV.) 'J'aime jouer à l'ordinateur.' (I like to play on the computer.) J'aime jouer au football.' (I like to play football.) 'J'aime la lecture.' (I like reading) 'J'aime écouter mes CDs.' (I like listening to my CDs.)

Further Activities

- Make block graphs to show the favourite class activities. Ask questions such as 'Combien d'enfants aiment faire de la gymnastique?' (How many children like doing gymnastics?)

- Ask the children to design CD covers for their favourite pop groups and practise saying 'J'aime écouter mes CDs.' (I like listening to my CDs.) 'J'aime écouter … (their favourite pop group and so on).'

- Make observational drawings of musical instruments and practise phrases such as 'Je joue de la flute à bec.' (I play the recorder.) or 'Natalie joue du piano.' (Natalie plays the piano.)

- Cut out pictures from magazines of people participating in various leisure activities. Mount on card and use them to ask 'Qu'est-ce qu'il/elle fait?' (What is he/she doing?) to elicit the response 'Il/elle joue au tennis …' (He/she is playing tennis …) and so on.

- Make clay models of figures participating in various activities and use these to practise phrases to do with sport.

Making the Display

- Make A3-sized pictures of sports and leisure activities using collage and paint. Mount these with the relevant French phrase underneath.

- Ask the children to draw each other in PE and gym lessons. Develop the sketches into black pen drawings on yellow paper. Display with the caption 'J'aime faire de la gymnastique.'

- Mount some of the block graphs and display alongside the pictures.

- Add a large label saying 'Qu'est-ce que vous aimez faire?'

Les Sports
Et
Les Loisirs

Conversation Model

- 'Qu'est-ce que tu aimes faire, Paul, le week-end?' (What do you like to do, Paul, at the weekend?)

- 'J'aime jouer au football le samedi matin.' (I like to play football on Saturday morning.)

- 'Moi, j'aime regarder le foot à la télévision le samedi après-midi!' (I like to watch football on the television on Saturday afternoon!)

- 'Samedi après-midi j'aime faire de l'équitation.' (I like to go horse riding on Saturday afternoon.)

- 'Qu'est-ce que tu aimes faire le soir?' (What do you like to do in the evening?)

- 'J'aime aller au cinéma ou à la discothèque.' (I like to go to the cinema or the disco.)

Vocabulary

J'aime jouer au football/au tennis …
    (I like to play football/tennis …)
J'aime jouer du piano/du violon/de la flûte à bec …
    (I like playing the piano/violin/recorder …)
J'aime regarder le snooker/le volleyball …
    (I like to watch snooker/volleyball …)
J'aime faire de la natation/de l'équitation/du vélo …
    (I like swimming/horse riding/cycling …)
J'aime aller au cinéma/au théâtre/à la discothèque …
    (I like to go to the cinema/theatre/disco …)
J'aime danser/dessiner/chanter …
    (I like dancing/drawing/singing …)

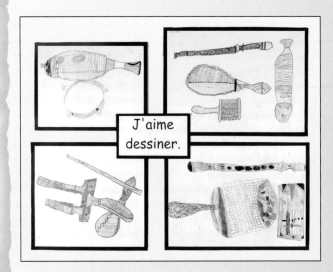

J'aime dessiner.

The Body (Le Corps)

Labels on the display: la tête, le cou, Le Corps, la main, les cheveux, l'épaule, le bras, le doigt, l'ongle, le front, l'oreille, le coude, les yeux, le nez, la taille, le pouce, la bouche, la hanche, le poignet, le genou, la jambe, le visage, la cheville, le pied

Starting Points

- Use classroom commands such as 'Levez-vous!' (Stand up!) 'Asseyez-vous.' (Sit down.) 'Levez la main.' (Put up your hand.) 'Baissez la main.' (Put your hand down.)

- Develop this into a game of 'Simon Says', matching commands to actions, such as 'Placez les mains sur la tête/sur les genoux/sur les épaules/sur les hanches.' (Put your hands on your head/knees/ shoulders/hips.) When the children are confident with several commands start to play the game properly, eliminating those who fail to respond correctly.

- Play a pencil and paper game. Draw the head and neck of an imaginary character. Fold the paper over to hide the drawing. Pass the paper onto the next person, who draws the shoulders, arms and top half of the character. Fold the paper over again and pass onto the next person, who draws the bottom half. Open up and see who has the oddest looking character. Use this game to practise phrases such as 'Dessinez la tête et les cheveux/les épaules et les bras/les jambes et les pieds.' (Draw the head and the hair/the shoulders and the arms/the legs and the feet.)

Further Activities

- Discuss body art and the way it is used in various cultures. Draw around the hand and cover in Mendhi patterns. Use such expressions as 'Coloriez les ongles en rouge.' (Colour the nails red.) Cut out the hands and mount on contrasting paper.

- Make 3-D hands by pouring plaster of Paris or casting plaster into rubber gloves. When the plaster has set, remove the glove very carefully to avoid breaking the fingers and then cover the hand in Mendhi patterns.

- Make large textile collages of faces and name the parts of the face.

- Set up a doctor's surgery in a corner of the classroom. Use this for class role-play to practise phrases such as 'Je ne me sens pas bien.' (I don't feel well.) 'Je me sens malade.' (I feel ill.) 'Asseyez-vous.' (Sit down.) 'Ouvrez la bouche.' (Open your mouth.) 'J'ai mal à la tête.' (I've got a headache.)

- Create clay sculptures (see picture on page 15). First form a face over a ball to give a 3-D effect. Next, cut out hand shapes from thinly rolled clay and join them, using slip, around the face to form hair. Paint or glaze when fired.

- Paint a figure wearing a vest and shorts, to fit the height of the display board. Place this centrally and label the parts of the body.

- Use one of the textile collages and label the facial features: le visage (face), les cheveux (hair), les yeux (eyes), un oeil (an eye), le nez (nose), la bouche (mouth), l'oreille (ear), le sourcil (eyebrow), le front (forehead), la joue (cheek), le menton (chin).

- Paint and cut out a large hand and label – la main (hand), le doigt (the finger), le pouce (the thumb), l'ongle (nail), l'articulation du doigt (knuckle), le poignet (wrist).

- Cut out some of the Mendhi patterned hands and position around the large hand.

Conversation Model

- 'Bonjour, Giselle.' (Hello, Giselle.)

- 'Bonjour, Martine.' (Hello, Martine.)

- 'Comment ça va aujourd'hui?' (How are you today?)

- 'Pas trop bien.' (Not very well.)

- 'Tu as mal à la tête?' (You've got a headache?)

- 'Non. J'ai mal à la gorge et mal à l'oreille.' (No. I've got a sore throat and earache.)

- 'Je ne me sens pas bien aussi.' (I don't feel well also.)

- 'Pourquoi?' (Why?)

- 'J'ai mal au ventre.' (I've got stomach ache.)

Vocabulary

la bouche (mouth)	le menton (chin)
le bras (arm)	le nez (nose)
les cheveux (hair)	l'orteil (toe)
la cheville (ankle)	le pied (foot)
le cou (neck)	le poignet (wrist)
le coude (elbow)	la poitrine (chest)
le doigt (finger)	le pouce (thumb)
l'épaule (shoulder)	le sourcil (eyebrow)
le genou (knee)	la taille (waist)
la hanche (hip)	la tête (head)
la jambe (leg)	le visage (face)
la joue (cheek)	les yeux (eyes)
la main (hand)	

Clothes (Les Vêtements)

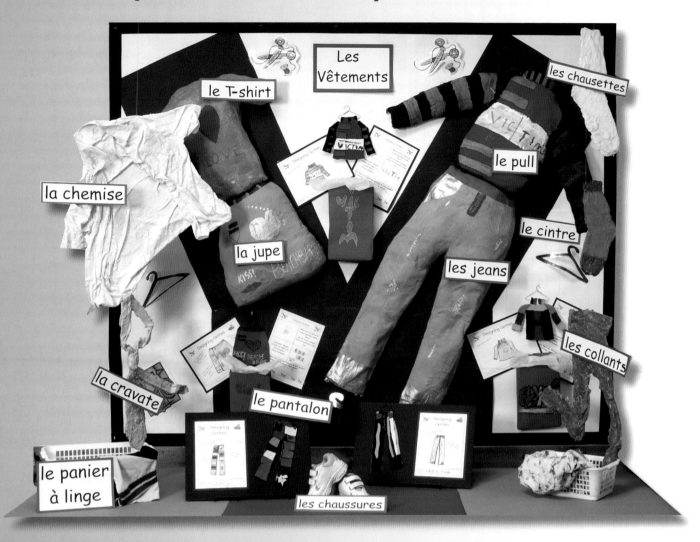

Starting Points

- Invite two children to stand in front of the class. Tell the class in French what they are wearing, item by item. 'Il porte un pantalon.' (He is wearing trousers.) 'Elle porte une jupe.' (She is wearing a skirt.) Say to the class 'Qu'est-ce qu'il porte?' (What is he wearing?) The children repeat 'Il porte un pantalon.' (He is wearing trousers.) Qu'est-ce qu'elle porte? (What is she wearing?) and so on.

- Extend to include colours. Show pictures of people wearing various colourful outfits and encourage the children to describe them. 'Elle porte un T-shirt jaune et un short rose.' (She is wearing a yellow T-shirt and pink shorts.)

- Make a collection of colourful hats, scarves, gloves and dressing-up clothes. The children could dress up and describe what they are wearing.

Further Activities

- Design seasonal outfits. Describe these, saying 'En hiver je porte …' (In winter I wear …) or 'En été je porte …' (In summer I wear …)

- Make card catwalks and models. Design and cut out outfits to fit on the models. Describe what they are wearing. 'Elle porte un pantalon en cuir noir.' (She is wearing black leather trousers.) 'Elle porte une robe en soie bleue.' (She is wearing a blue silk dress.')

- Cut out pictures from magazines and catalogues and mount them on card. Print out separate matching descriptions and use these for group activities. One child holds up a picture and says 'Qu'est-ce qu'il porte?' Another child finds the matching sentence and reads it out loud.

Making the Display

- Cover the display board and table with brightly coloured paper.

- Stuff child-size garments with crumpled paper to give form. Wrap the stuffed garments with clingfilm so that they are completely protected and then wrap with Modroc. When the Modroc has set, carefully remove the paper and the garment and paint the model.

- Suspend the finished models with nylon line from the ceiling in front of the display board or attach them to the board.

- Arrange clothes in a plastic basket to represent an overflowing laundry basket. Add shoes and boots, gloves, scarf and hat.

- Add labels and the children's designs.

Conversation Model

- 'Qu'est-ce que tu vas porter ce soir?' (What are you going to wear tonight?)

- 'Je vais porter mon pantalon noir.' (I'm going to wear my black trousers.)

- 'Ton pantalon noir! Moi, je vais porter une jupe.' (Your black trousers! I'm going to wear a skirt.)

- 'Quelle jupe?' (Which skirt?)

- 'La verte.' (The green one.)

- 'Je vais porter mon pantalon et un chemisier rouge.' (I'm going to wear my trousers and a red blouse.)

Vocabulary

les bottes (boots)	la fermeture éclair (zip fastener)
la boucle (buckle)	
le bouton (button)	les gants (gloves)
la ceinture (belt)	l'imperméable (raincoat)
le chapeau (hat)	le jean (jeans)
les chaussettes (socks)	le manteau (coat)
les chaussures (shoes)	le pull (pullover)
la chemise (shirt)	la robe (dress)
le chemisier (blouse)	le tricot (knitted jumper)
les collants (tights)	les sandales (sandals)
la cravate (tie)	la veste (jacket)
l'écharpe (scarf)	

Pets (Les Animaux Familiers)

Starting Points

- Ask the children with pets to bring in photographs of them. Using flashcards of pictures of pets with their names in French underneath, practise questions and answers. 'Qu'est-ce que c'est?' 'C'est une tortue.' (What is this? It's a tortoise.) 'Qui as un animal?'/'As-tu un animal?' 'J'ai un chien.' (Who has an animal?/Do you have an animal? I have a dog.)

- In ICT, use graphics programs to design and print out simple lotto cards with pictures of pets and their names. Use these in the French lessons to play lotto. Call out random pets and the first child to get a row of four becomes the new caller.

Further Activities

- Create different kinds of pets using modelling materials and textile techniques. For example, stuff and decorate the legs of old tights to create snakes or make wool pom-poms as mice or birds. Practise phrases such as 'Je fait un serpent.' (I am making a snake.) 'Je fait une petite souris.' (I am making a little mouse.)

- Draw tropical fish on card and colour both sides. Hang the fish from dowel or wire placed across the top of an aquarium, or create an aquarium by cutting rectangular holes in the sides of a cardboard carton and covering it with clear plastic. Ask questions such as 'Il y a combien de poissons?' (How many fish are there?)

- Make life-size papier-mâché dogs and cats, using chicken wire or packaging material as a base. Alternatively, stuff crumpled newspaper into a large plastic bag, divide the shape into a head and body by tying with string and cover with Modroc. Describe the models: 'Mon chien est grand et noir.' (My dog is big and black.)

- Make simple fur fabric cats by gathering up, stuffing and sewing together circles of fabric. Add eyes, ears, nose and tail.

Conversation Model

- 'As-tu un animal familier?' (Have you got a pet?)

- 'Oui, j'ai un chat.' (Yes, I've got a cat.)

- 'Quel âge a-t-il?' (How old is it?)

- 'Il a trois ans.' (It's three years old.)

- 'De quelle couleur est-il?' (What colour is it?)

- 'Il est noir.' (It's black.)

Making the Display

- Create a pet shop display. Make a perch by suspending a long tube on strips of coloured paper. On this, display model birds made from sections of egg cartons and feathers.

- Make cages from shoeboxes and cartons. Add a little hay and the children's animals. Staple the cages or pet boxes to the display board to look as if they are on shelves. Add actual bird or hamster cages if available. Supplement the display with soft toys if necessary.

- Place one of the model dogs in a pet basket or bed. Add pet leads, collars and bowls.

- Add tins and packets of pet food. Label the display.

Vocabulary

l'aquarium (aquarium)
la boîte (box)
le chat (cat)
le chaton (kitten)
le chien (dog)
le chiot (puppy)
le clapier (rabbit hutch)
le cochon d'Inde (Guinea pig)
le jardin (garden)

le lapin (rabbit)
la niche (kennel)
le panier du chien (dog basket)
la perruche (budgerigar)
le poisson rouge (goldfish)
le poney (pony)
le serpent (snake)
la souris (mouse)
la tortue (tortoise)

My Daily Routine (Ma Routine Journalière)

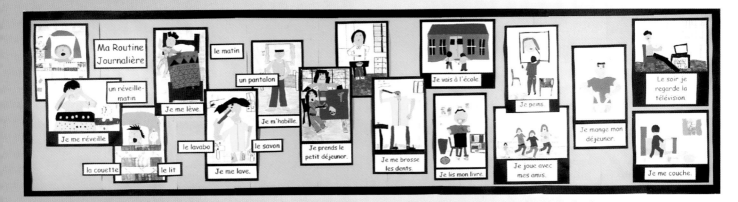

Starting Points

- Ask the children what time they get up in the morning. 'À quelle heure est-ce que tu te lèves le matin?' 'Je me lève à sept heures.' (I get up at seven o'clock.)

- When the children are confident saying what time they get up, introduce phrases such as 'Je me lave.' (I get washed.) 'Je m'habille.' (I get dressed.)

- Ask the children to describe their daily routine.

Further Activities

- Fold an A3 sheet of drawing paper into eight sections. Cartoon style, draw a daily activity in each of the sections, complete with captions in French: 'Je me lève' and so on. The children could take it in turns to read out their cartoon sheet.

- Cut some of the cartoon sheets into eight sections and mount the pieces on card to make playing cards. The aim of the game is to collect a complete daily routine.

- Play miming games, in which one child mimes an action from the daily routine and the others have to guess what he/she is doing. 'Il se brosse les dents.' (He is brushing his teeth.) 'Elle se lave.' (She is washing.) and so on.

Conversation Model

- 'À quelle heure tu te lèves, Richard?' (What time do you get up, Richard?)

- 'Moi, je me lève à sept heures trente. À quelle heure tu te lèves?' (I get up at seven-thirty. What time do you get up?)

- 'Je me lève à sept heures.' (I get up at seven o'clock.)

- 'Tu quittes la maison à quelle heure?' (What time do you leave the house?)

- 'Je quitte la maison à huit heures vingt.' (I leave the house at twenty past eight.)

- 'Tu prends le bus?' (Do you catch the bus?)

- 'Oui. Je prends le bus à huit heures trente.' (Yes. I catch the bus at eight-thirty.)

Making the Display

- Taking inspiration from the daily routine cartoon sheets, create A3 collages using a wide variety of coloured papers. Add background detail in felt-tip pen and coloured pencil. Make a collage for each of the key phrases.

- Mount the collages on black paper with the printed phrase underneath.

- Position all the pictures on the display board in the order of the daily routine.

- Add vocabulary which relates to the individual pieces of artwork, such as le lit (the bed), la couverture (the cover), le lavabo (the washbasin).

Je lis mon livre.

Je vais à l'école.

Vocabulary

Je me réveille. (I wake up.)
Je me lève. (I get up.)
Je me lave. (I get washed.)
Je m'habille. (I get dressed.)
Je prends le petit déjeuner. (I have my breakfast.)
Je me brosse les dents. (I brush my teeth.)
Je quitte la maison. (I leave the house.)
Je vais à l'école. (I go to school.)
J'écris. (I write.)
Je lis mon livre. (I read my book.)
Je peins. (I paint.)
Je joue avec mes amis. (I play with my friends.)
Je prends mon déjeuner. (I have my lunch.)
Je rentre chez-moi. (I come home.)
Je regarde la télévision. (I watch the television.)
Je me couche. (I go to bed.)

A Day at School (Un Jour à l'École)

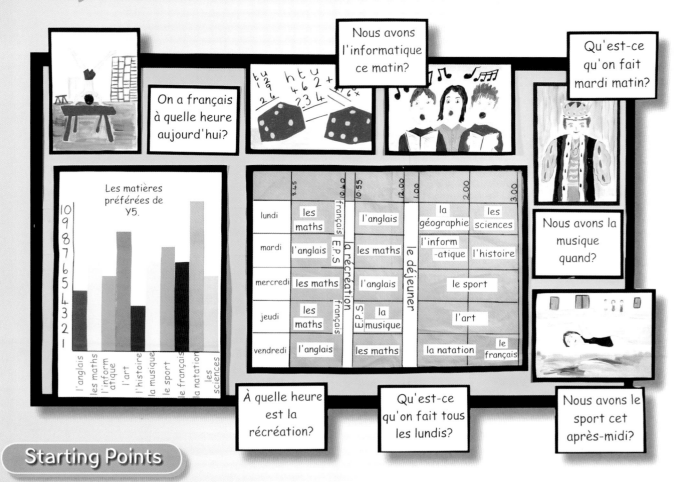

Starting Points

- Ask the children to make a list in English of all the activities they do in a week, then draw a picture of their favourite activity. Ask them 'Quelle est ta matière préférée?' (What is your favourite subject?) Each child in turn holds up his/her picture and repeats after you 'Ma matière préférée est l'anglais/la musique/le sport …' (My favourite subject is English/Music/Sport …) Practise this until the children are familiar with all the different subjects.

- Display a large timetable of the week's activities and ask the children to take turns in saying which subject they have on the different days of the week, for example 'Lundi matin j'ai les mathématiques et l'anglais.' (Monday morning I have Maths and English.)

- Relate telling the time to the class timetable, for example 'On a français à quelle heure aujourd'hui?' (What time do we have French today?) 'À dix heures? À dix heures quinze?' (At ten o'clock? At ten-fifteen?)

Further Activities

- Make a large block graph to show the children's favourite school subjects. Use it to ask questions such as 'L'anglais est la matière préférée de combien d'enfants?' (How many children like English best?)

- Make small flashcards to illustrate the subjects. Have the names of the subjects written on separate cards. Play picture and sentence matching games and memory games in small groups.

- In ICT, make posters to advertise after-school clubs and activities in French, stating place and time.
- Carry out a 'sondage loisirs' (leisure survey) to see what activities the children would like to do after school if there was the opportunity.

Conversation Model

- 'On a musique à quelle heure aujourd'hui?' (What time do we have Music today?)
- 'Cet après-midi à deux heure. J'aime la musique.' (This afternoon at two o'clock. I like Music.)
- 'J'aime la musique mais ma matière préféré est les mathématiques.' (I like Music but my favourite subject is Maths.)
- 'Je n'aime pas les mathématiques.' (I don't like Maths.)
- 'Quelle est ta matiére préférée?' (What is your favourite subject?)
- 'Les sciences. C'est intéressant.' (Science. It's interesting.)

Vocabulary

l'appel (the register)
Le dessin (drawing)
le déjeuner (lunchtime)
l'éducation physique et sportive (Physical Education)
l'espagnol (Spanish)
le français (French)
La géographie (Geography)
la gymnastique (Gymnastics)
l'histoire (History)
l'informatique (ICT)
les mathématiques (Mathematics)
las musique (Music)
la peinture (painting)
la récréation (break time)
les sciences (Science)
C'est intéressant. (It's interesting.)
C'est ennuyeux. (It's boring.)
J'aime. (I like.)
Je n'aime pas. (I don't like.)
tous les jours (every day)
tous les lundis (every Monday)
le lundi (on Monday)

Making the Display

- Make a large, colourful class timetable in French and place in the centre of the display board, surrounded by questions and statements, such as 'On a quelle matière le mardi matin avant la récréation?' (What subject do we have on Tuesday morning before break?) or 'La gymnastique est à onze heures vendredi matin.' (Gymastics is at eleven o'clock on Friday morning.)

- Paint pictures to illustrate each of the subjects and mount with the appropriate captions. Display these around the timetable, leaving a space for the large block graph.

- If there is room on the display board, add some of the posters advertising the after-school clubs and the results of the survey.

In the Classroom (Dans la Classe)

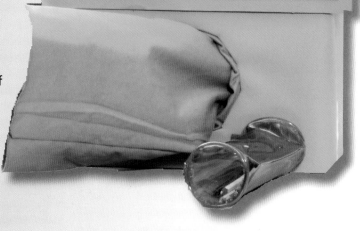

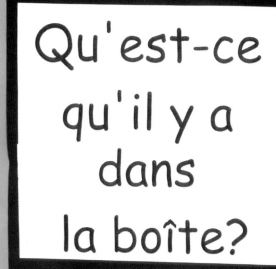

Qu'est-ce qu'il y a dans la boîte?

Starting Points

- Move around the classroom picking up and pointing to objects in the room, saying, for example, 'C'est un crayon! Qu'est-ce que c'est?' (This is a crayon! What is it?) to elicit a response. Repeat with other objects. When the class is confident, ask the same questions of individual children.

- Play the game 'Je pense à un objet qui commence par T.' (I think of an object beginning with T.) The children take turns to guess, using a whole phrase. For example, 'C'est une table?', to which the response is either 'Oui. C'est une table.' or 'Non. Ce n'est pas une table.' (Is this a table?/ Yes. It's a table./No. It's not a table.) This practises the negative form.

Further Activities

- Play the game 'Je pense à quelque chose. Qu'est-ce que c'est?' (I'm thinking of something. What is it?) The children take turns to ask questions, such as 'De quelle couleur est-ce?' (What colour is it?) 'C'est grand?' (Is it big?) 'C'est petit?' (Is it small?) 'C'est en bois/plastique/métal/verre/caoutchouc?' (Is it made of wood/plastic/metal/glass/rubber?)

- Make a 'feely bag' or use a box with a hand-sized hole cut in the side. Place objects in this and let the children feel them and describe what they are touching, for example, 'C'est très petit. C'est en caoutchouc. C'est une gomme!' (It's very small. It's made of rubber. It's an eraser!)

- Make sets of cards with pictures of classroom objects so that the children can work in groups to play 'Happy Families', 'Four of a Kind', 'Snap' or 'Remembrance', practising phrases such as 'As-tu un livre?' 'Oui, j'ai de livre.' 'Voici un livre.' 'Non, je n'ai pas un livre.' 'Passe-moi le livre, s'il te plaît.' (Have you got a book? Yes, I have a book. Here's a book. No, I've not got a book. Pass me the book please.)

Conversation Model

- 'Sylvie! Je n'ai pas de stylo!' (Sylvie! I haven't got a pen!)

- 'Pourquoi pas?' (Why not?)

- 'J'ai laissé ma trousse à la maison.' (I left my pencil case at home.)

- 'Voici un stylo.' (Here's a pen.)

- 'Merci beaucoup.' (Thank you very much.)

Making the Display

- Paint/colour pictures of classroom objects, such as a pencil case, a ruler, a pencil sharpener, a book and so on, making some much larger than life.

- Cut out the image, then cut it into several pieces either randomly or into jigsaw piece shapes. Jumble up the pieces and mount on contrasting coloured paper. Ask the children to guess what the image is. 'Qu'est-ce que c'est?' (What is this?)

- Cut out some images and mount on stiff card. Glue a small box or packet to the back of it so as to create a 3-D effect when mounted.

- Place the 'feely bag' filled with light objects, some soft, some hard, in the centre of the display surrounded by the questions.

C'est un sac.

Vocabulary

un cahier (exercise book)
un cartable (school bag)
une chaise (chair)
un crayon (pencil)
un crayon de couleur (coloured pencil)
une fenêtre (window)
une feuille de papier (sheet of paper)
un feutre (felt-tipped pen)

une gomme (rubber)
un livre (book)
un ordinateur (computer)
une porte (door)
une règle (ruler)
un rideau (curtain)
un sac (bag)
un stylo (pen)
un taille-crayon (pencil sharpener)
une trousse (pencil case)

The Weather (Le Temps)

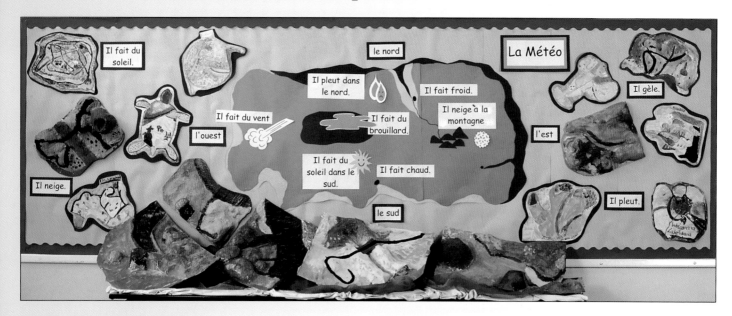

Labels on display: Il fait du soleil. · le nord · La Météo · Il pleut dans le nord. · Il fait froid. · Il gèle. · Il fait du vent · l'ouest · Il fait du brouillard. · Il neige à la montagne · l'est · Il fait du soleil dans le sud. · Il fait chaud. · Il neige. · le sud · Il pleut.

Starting Points

- Ask the children what the weather is like today. 'Quel temps fait-il aujourd'hui?' Keep a daily weather chart using illustrated flashcards. Change the cards as the weather changes throughout the day. You might start with 'Il fait beau.' (It's fine.), but an hour later it could change to 'Il pleut.' (It's raining.), while in the afternoon it could be 'Il y a du soleil.' (It's sunny.)

- The children make their own larger illustrated flashcards for each of the weather phrases and use these in groups to practise the question and answer routine, for example, 'Quel temps fait-il?'/'Il fait mauvais.' (What's the weather like?/The weather's bad.)

Further Activities

- Collect pictures from magazines and travel catalogues illustrating different kinds of weather and mount them on card to make picture and sentence matching games.

- Design symbols to represent the different types of weather. Draw imaginary island maps with physical features, such as mountains, rivers, lakes and forests, and mark the weather symbols on the map. The children present their own 'la météo' (weather forecast): 'Dans le nord il fait beau mais dans l'ouest il pleut.' (In the north it's fine, but in the west it's raining.) and so on.

- Make a collection of clothes and articles, such as hats, scarves, sunglasses, umbrellas, large wellington boots, plastic rainmacs and empty suntan lotion containers. Allow the children to dress up and ask the class 'Quel temps fait-il?' (What's the weather like?), changing quickly from one type of clothing to another. Also use the dressing-up clothes when presenting the weather forecast.

- Make relief islands from crumpled-up newspaper and papier mâché on a carton-card base. Discuss the location of the imaginary islands and create a weather forecast in French.

Conversation Model

- 'Bonjour, Marie. Quel beau jour!' (Hello, Marie. What a beautiful day!)

- 'Oui, il fait du soleil.' (Yes, it's sunny.)

- 'Il fait du vent aussi.' (It's also windy.)

- 'Oui, mais j'ai chaud.' (Yes, but I'm hot.)

- 'Moi aussi. Au revoir.' (Me too. Goodbye.)

- 'Au revoir, Jean.' (Goodbye, John.)

Making the Display

- Using the children's island pictures for inspiration, cut out an island shape from green display paper and position on the board. Add touches of yellow paper here and there for sandy beaches.

- Add features such as mountains, forests, rivers and lakes and mark in imaginary towns.

- Cut out and position some of the children's islands in the sea around the main island.

- Make large, clear weather symbols using stiff card and then laminate them. These can be positioned on the display with Blu-tack and repositioned when the children are presenting the weather forecast.

- Print out clear labels for all the weather vocabulary and laminate on stiff card. Attach with Blu-tack for repositioning.

- Place the painted relief islands in front of the main display.

Vocabulary

Il fait chaud. (It's hot.)
Il fait froid. (It's cold.)
Il neige. (It's snowing.)
Il gèle. (It's freezing.)
Il fait du vent. (It's windy.)
Il fait du brouillard. (It's foggy.)
Il y a des nuages. (It's cloudy.)
Il pleut. (It's raining)
J'ai chaud. (I am hot.)
J'ai froid. (I am cold.)

Colours (Les Couleurs)

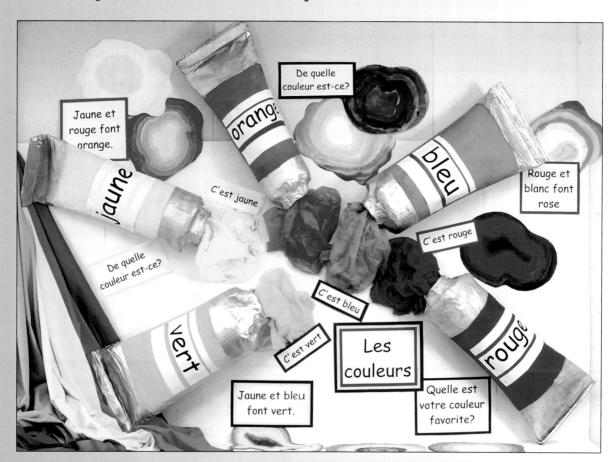

De quelle couleur est-ce?

Jaune et rouge font orange.

orange

jaune

C'est jaune

bleu

Rouge et blanc font rose

C'est rouge

De quelle couleur est-ce?

C'est bleu

vert

C'est vert

Les couleurs

rouge

Jaune et bleu font vert.

Quelle est votre couleur favorite?

Starting Points

- Show the children a variety of coloured objects, holding each one up in turn and saying 'C'est la couleur jaune/bleu/rouge …' (This is the colour yellow/blue/red …) Pose the question: 'De quelle couleur est-ce?' (What colour is it?) The children reply 'C'est jaune.' (It's yellow.) Ask each child what their favourite colour is: 'Quelle est ta couleur favorite?', to which they reply 'C'est rouge.' (It's red.) and so on.

- Play the game 'Je pense à quelque chose dans la classe. Qu'est-ce que c'est?' (I'm thinking of something in the class. What is it?) The children pose the questions: 'De quelle couleur est-ce?' 'C'est grand?' 'C'est petit?' (What colour is it? Is it big? Is it small?)

Further Activities

C'est rouge

- Practise colour mixing. Add very small quantities of a colour at a time to white to see how many shades can be created. Use phrases such as 'Bleu et jaune font vert.' (Blue and yellow make green.) 'Rouge et blanc font rose.' (Red and white make pink.)

- Weave small panels in a chosen colour, incorporating as many different shades, textures and materials as possible. Practise naming the colours in French.

- For the display, make very large models of paint tubes by rolling up lengths of chicken wire. Flatten and roll over one end of the roll of wire to create the bottom of the paint tube and shape the open end into the neck of the tube. Paste the shape with white paper and when dry, paint to resemble a tube of paint.

Conversation Model

- 'Quelle est ta couleur favorite?' (What's your favourite colour?)

- 'C'est bleu.' (It's blue.)

- 'Moi, j'aime jaune.' (I love yellow.)

- 'Ma chambre est jaune, mais je préfére bleu.' (My bedroom is yellow, but I prefer blue.)

- 'Ma chambre est jaune claire. C'est superbe!' (My bedroom is light yellow. It's wonderful!)

Making the Display

- Drape lengths of blue, green, yellow, orange and red different-textured fabric at one end of the display area, allowing the fabric to flow onto a work surface or table. Scatter large coloured sequins onto the fabric.

- Arrange the model paint tubes around the board as if it were a palette, stapling the tubes to the board from the inside.

- Crumple up coloured tissue paper to represent the paint oozing out of the tubes. Push it into the open ends of the tubes.

- Trim the colour mixing work into irregular shapes and disperse between the mounted tubes.

- Add labels 'De quelle couleur est-ce?' and 'C'est rouge.' and so on.

Vocabulary

blanc(he) (white)
bleu(e) (blue)
brun(e) (brown)
clair(e) (light)
foncé (dark)
gris(e) (grey)
jaune (yellow)
noir (black)
rouge (red)
vert(e) (green)

The Seasons (Les Saisons)

LES SAISONS

le printemps

mars
avril
mai

les fleurs

l'oiseau

les feuilles

l'été

juin
juillet
août

l'automne

septembre
octobre
novembre

le chapeau

les vêtements d'hiver

l'hiver

l'arbre

décembre
janvier
février

l'écharpe

les mitaines

les gants

les bottes de caoutchouc

Starting Points

- Discuss the current season, talking about the months, the weather and the particular characteristics of that season. Introduce the French words for that season and the months that comprise it.

- Make flashcards illustrating the four seasons and use these with the weather flashcards (see page 26). 'En automne il y a du vent.' (In autumn it's windy.) 'En hiver il gèle.' (In winter it freezes.) and so on.

Further Activities

- Use twisted newspaper, paint, coloured papers, tissue, string and other collage materials to create pictures of trees through the seasons. Label 'un arbre en automne' or 'un arbre au printemps' and so on.

- Press large leaves with deep veins into rolled, self-hardening clay. Cut around the leaf and prop up the edges with crumpled newspaper until it dries out. Paint the desired colour and label 'une feuille d'automne' (an autumn leaf) and so on.

- Collage seasonal pictures using fabric and display with relevant captions, such as 'En été il fait du soleil.' (In summer it's sunny.) 'En hiver il fait froid.' (In winter it's cold.)

Making the Display

- Cover the display board with pale blue paper.

- Bind three lengths of carpet tube together to create a tree trunk. Glue twisted lengths of newspaper to this to create texture or staple corrugated card around the tubes. Draw the tree branches on stiff paper or card and cut out. Paint the trunk and branches. When dry, staple the top half of the tree to the tree trunk. Staple the ends of the branches to the display board.

- Paint leaves or make leaf-prints in autumn colours and cut out. Position these in the autumn section of the display to look as if they are falling.

- Cut out summer leaves from different shades of green paper or ask the children to draw around and cut out their hand shapes. Overlap these to build up a thick foliage.

- Collage nest shapes using carton card and straw, raffia or hay. Add painted birds.

- Glue different shades of crumpled pink tissue to a background shape for the springtime blossom.

- Rumple up a length of white silky fabric to the side of the tree to represent the snow and prop a sledge against the tree.

- Display a collection of winter clothing and labels.

Conversation Model

- 'Bonjour, Danielle. Il fait froid, n'est-ce pas?' (Hello, Danielle. It's cold, isn't it?)

- 'Oui, c'est automne.' (Yes, it's autumn.)

- 'J'aime les feuilles en automne.' (I like the leaves in autumn.)

- 'Oui, elles sont jaunes et rouges.' (Yes, they're yellow and red.)

- 'J'aime le mois d'octobre.' (I like the month of October.)

- 'Moi aussi. À bientôt!' (Me too. See you soon!)

- 'À bientôt, Danielle.' (See you soon, Danielle.)

Vocabulary

l'arbre/les arbres (the tree(s))
brun(e) (brown)
la feuille/les feuilles (the leaf/leaves)
la fleur/les fleurs (the flower(s))
jaune (yellow)
l'oiseau/les oiseaux (the bird(s))
rouge (red)
vert(e) (green)

janvier (January), février (February), mars (March), avril (April), mai (May), juin (June), juillet (July), août (August), septembre (September), octobre (October), novembre (November), décembre (December)

au printemps (in the spring)
en été (in the summer)
en automne (in the autumn)
en hiver (in the winter)

les vêtements d'hiver
le chapeau
les mitaines
l'écharpe
les gants

What Time Is It? (Quelle Heure Est-Il?)

Starting Points

- Count up to 60 in French and practise counting forwards and backwards in fives. Show the children a large clock face and count round the clock. The children take turns in moving the hands to the different hours and asking the class 'Quelle heure est-il?' They choose someone to answer 'Il est sept heures.' (It's seven o'clock.) and so on.

- Introduce the quarters and the half hour. For example, 'Il est neuf heures moins le quart.' (It's a quarter to nine.) 'Il est neuf heures et quart.' (It's a quarter past nine.) 'Il est neuf heures et demie.' (It's half-past nine.)

- Introduce the minutes past the hour: 'Il est neuf heures cinq/dix/ quinze/vingt/vingt-cinq/trente.' (It is five/ten/fifteen/twenty/twenty-five/thirty past nine.)

- Introduce the minutes to the hour: 'Il est dix heures moins vingt-cinq/vingt/quinze/dix/cinq.' (It is twenty-five/twenty/fifteen/ten/five to ten.)

Further Activities

- Relate telling the time to the daily routine (see pages 20–21). 'Vous arrivez à l'école à quelle heure?' (What time do you arrive at school?) 'J'arrive à neuf heures moins le quart.' (I arrive at a quarter to nine.) Draw pictures of the daily routine and label accordingly. 'Je me lève à sept heures et demie.' (I get up at half-past seven.)

- Make time collages of clocks cut out from catalogues and magazines with the correct times written underneath.

- Cut out clock faces from magazines and catalogues and adapt to illustrate minutes past and to the hour. Make corresponding sentences and play question and answer games in small groups.

Conversation Model

- 'Bonjour, Alain!' (Good day, Alan!)

- 'Bonjour, Philipe. Tu es en retard!' (Good day, Philip. You're late!)

- 'Pourquoi? Quelle heure est-il?' (Why? What time is it?)

- 'Il est dix heures et quart.' (It's a quarter past ten.)

- 'Ma montre retarde.' (My watch is slow.)

- 'Ta montre retarde de quinze minutes!' (Your watch is fifteen minutes slow!)

Il est six heures.
Quelle heure est-il?
Quelle heure est-il?
Il est deux heures moins dix.
Quelle heure est-il?
Il est dix heures dix.
Quelle heure est-il?
Il est onze heures cinq.

Making the Display

- Design a clock for a clock shop display. The clocks can vary from a small travel clock to a large grandfather clock. Design nets of the basic shape, cut out of card and assemble. Alternatively, make a collection of empty boxes of various sizes and use these as the basic clock shape.

- Paint or collage the front of the clock and the face and attach to the box. Collage the shopkeeper.

- Add labels telling the times shown on the clock.

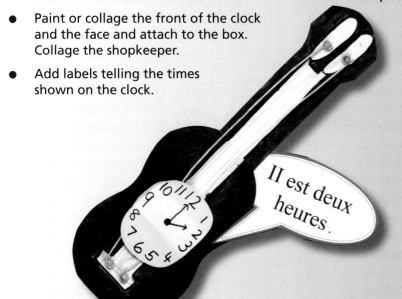

Il est deux heures.

Vocabulary

les aiguilles (hands of a clock)
une demi-heure (half an hour)
une heure (hour)
une horloge (clock)
une minute (minute)
une montre (watch)
un quart d'heure (quarter of an hour)
un réveille-matin (alarm clock)
à ma montre (by my watch)
être en retard (to be late)
tôt (early)

The House (La Maison)

Starting Points

- Encourage the children to talk about their own homes. Find out which is their favourite room in the house and why. Collect pictures from magazines illustrating the different rooms of the house and ask 'C'est quelle pièce?' (Which room is it?) 'C'est la chambre.' (It's the bedroom.) 'C'est la cuisine.' (It's the kitchen.) and so on.

Further Activities

- Draw floor plans of houses, labelling the rooms. Use these to describe the layout of the house, for example, 'La salle de séjour est à gauche en face de la salle à manger.' Working in pairs, the children ask questions, for example, 'Où est la salle de bains?' (Where is the bathroom?), replying 'En haut, à droite.' (Upstairs, on the right.)

- Ask the children to imagine they are selling a house. Draw a picture and compose a simple description. 'Petite maison. Rez-de-chaussée (l'entrée, salle de séjour, cuisine). Premier étage (deux chambres, salle de bains). Petit jardin.' (Small house. Ground floor [entrance, living room, kitchen]. First floor [two bedrooms, bathroom]. Small garden.) Set up an estate agent's office in the corner of the classroom.

- In Design and Technology, create model rooms using cardboard boxes. Cut out windows and doors. Line the walls with wallpaper and cover the floors with furnishing fabrics. Ask 'Qu'est que tu fais?' (What are you making?) 'Je fais une salle de séjour avec une porte-fenêtre.' (I'm making a living room with French windows.) Join some of the rooms together to create dolls' houses. Use for giving directions about the house.

- Create doll's house furniture from small boxes and junk materials.

Conversation Model

- 'Quelle est ta pièce favorite?' (Which is your favourite room?)

- 'C'est la salle de séjour.' (It's the living room.)

- 'Pourquoi?' (Why?)

- 'Parce que nous regardons la télévision là.' (Because we watch the television there.)

- 'Moi, je regarde la télévision dans ma chambre. J'adore ma chambre.' (I watch the television in my bedroom. I love my bedroom.)

- 'J'ai mon ordinateur dans ma chambre.' (I have my computer in my bedroom.)

Making the Display

- Working in twos, ask the children to draw and paint large pictures of the rooms of the house.

- Mount these on the display board to look like a house with the front removed.

- Separate the rooms with strips of black paper.

- Cut out and add a roof.

- Add labels mounted on black paper.

Vocabulary

l'armoire (wardrobe)
la baignoire (bath)
le buffet (dresser/sideboard)
le canapé (sofa)
la cave (cellar)
la chambre (bedroom)
la commode (chest of drawers)
la cuisine (kitchen)
la cuisinière (cooker)
la douche (shower)
l'entrée (entrance hall)
l'évier (sink)
le fauteuil (armchair)
le frigidaire (fridge)
le grand lit (double bed)
le grenier (attic)
le lavabo (washbasin)
le lit (bed)
le premier étage (first floor)
le rez-de-chaussée (ground floor)
la salle à manger (dining room)
la salle de bains (bathroom)
la salle de séjour (living room)
la télévision (television)
les toilettes (toilet)

In the Garden (Dans le Jardin)

Starting Points

- Ask the class to tell you about their own gardens or gardens that they have visited or seen on the television. Ask them to draw pictures of what they would like to put in their ideal garden. Use the discussion and pictures to introduce the vocabulary, for example, 'Qu'est-ce que c'est?' 'C'est un arbre.' (What is it? It's a tree.) 'Qu'est-ce que c'est?' 'C'est la pelouse.' (What is it? It's the lawn.)

- Ask if anyone helps in the garden at home. 'Qui aime faire le jardinage?' (Who likes to do the gardening?) 'J'aime arroser les fleurs.' (I like to water the flowers.) 'Je balaye le chemin.' (I sweep the path.) 'Mon père/Ma mère coupe l'herbe.' (My father/mother cuts the grass.)

Further Activities

- 'Semez des graines'. Sow some seeds and watch them grow. Sow cress seeds on damp cotton wool in washed-out eggshells. Draw faces on the shells and the growing seeds will appear as hair.

- Make paper or fabric collages of gardens by cutting out flowers and images from wallpaper, furnishing fabrics and magazines. Ask the children to describe their collages. 'Voici une pelouse.' (Here is a lawn.) 'Voici des fleurs.' (Here are some flowers.)

- Look at different types of water features and design a wall-mounted water feature to look like a face, gargoyle or green man and make from clay.

Conversation Model

- 'As-tu un jardin?' (Have you got a garden?)

- 'Oui. J'ai un petit jardin.' (Yes. I've got a small garden.)

- 'As-tu une pelouse?' (Have you got a lawn?)

- 'Oui. J'ai une pelouse et des parterres.' (Yes. I've got a lawn and some flower beds.)

- 'As-tu une serre?' (Have you got a greenhouse?)

- 'Non, mais j'ai un très petit abris jardin.' (No, but I've got a very small garden shed.)

le jet d'eau

Making the Display

- Make one side of a garden shed from carton card and position on the display board.

- Stand a branch in a plant pot or staple it to the board and decorate with leaves made from paper.

- Place a table or cupboard in front of the display board and cover with imitation grass, a green cloth or green paper. On this, arrange a selection of garden tools and small plant pots.

- Create flowers and plants from junk and modelling materials and add to the display to create a garden.

- Choose one of the water features and position on the 'wall' of the display.

- Add appropriate labels.

Vocabulary

l'abris jardin (garden shed)
l'arbre (tree)
le balai (sweeping brush)
la bêche (spade)
la binette (hoe)
la brouette (wheelbarrow)
les feuilles (leaves)
la fleur (flower)
la fourche (fork)
les graines (seeds)
la haie (hedge)
le parterre (flower bed)
la pelle (shovel)
la pelouse (lawn)
les plantes (plants)
le râteau (rake)
la serre (greenhouse)
la tondeuse (lawnmower)
la truelle (trowel)
un ver de terre (worm)

Helping Around the House (Aider à la Maison)

Je passe l'aspirateur.

Je mets la table.

Je fais la vaisselle.

Je fais les courses.

Je fais les vitres.

Que faites-vous pour aider à la maison?

Je coupe l'herbe.

Starting Points

- Ask the class what they do to help around the house: 'Qu'est-ce que tu fais pour aider à la maison?' Make a list of the kind of jobs that they could do. Show them pictures of people doing household chores. 'Qu'est-ce qu'il/elle fait?' (What is he/she doing?) 'Il/elle lave la voiture.' (He/she is washing the car.) and so on.

Qu'est-ce qu'il faut faire pour ranger la pièce?

Further Activities

- Ask each child to draw a picture of their bedroom in a very untidy state: bed unmade, clothes, books and toys on the floor, dirty mugs and plates lying around and so on. Ask them what must be done to tidy the room: 'Qu'est-ce qu'il faut faire pour ranger la pièce?'

- Play miming games where the children have to guess which household chore is being mimed. Ask 'Qu'est-ce qu'il fait?' (What is he doing?) 'Il essuie la vaisselle.' (He's drying the dishes.)

- Collect pictures of people performing household tasks. Mount these on card and provide matching sentences. In small groups, ask the children to match the sentence to the activity, saying the sentence out loud as they do so. Alternatively, one child holds up the pictures in turn and asks the group 'Qu'est-ce qu'il fait?' Someone in the group then selects the correct matching sentence.

Conversation Model

- 'Qu'est-ce que tu fais pour aider à la maison?' (What do you do to help around the house?)

- 'Je fais mon lit. Qu'est-ce que tu fais?' (I make my bed. What do you do?)

- 'Je mets la table.' (I set the table)

- 'Je débarrasse la table.' (I clear the table.)

- 'Je fais la vaisselle.' (I wash the dishes.)

- 'Nous avons un lave-vaisselle!' (We have a dishwasher!)

Making the Display

- Paint or collage a large picture of a very untidy room. Place this in the centre of the display board with the caption 'Que fais-tu pour aider à la maison?' (What do you do to help around the house?)

- Paint or collage smaller pictures representing a range of household chores. Mount these with the appropriate caption underneath and arrange around the centre picture.

- Make a display of household items, such as an ironing board (une planche à repasser), an iron (un fer à repasser), a vacuum cleaner (un aspirateur), a bucket (un seau), une serpillière (floor cloth), a duster (un chiffon), a sweeping brush (un balai), a lawnmower (une tondeuse), a small stepladder (un escabeau), and label them appropriately.

Vocabulary

Je fais la vaisselle. (I do the dishes.)
Je passe l'aspirateur. (I do the vacuum cleaning.)
Je range ma chambre. (I tidy my bedroom.)
Je fais les courses. (I do the shopping.)
Je fais le jardinage. (I do the gardening.)
Je coupe l'herbe. (I cut the grass.)
Je fais les vitres. (I do the windows.)
J'essuie la vaisselle. (I dry the dishes.)
Je fais le repassage. (I do the ironing.)

The Kitchen (La Cuisine)

la poêle

La Cuisine

la planche à repasser

le grille-pain

LA LESSIVE

le fer à repasser

la casserole

la bouilloire

Qu'est- ce qu'il y a dans le placard?

la machine à laver

Starting Points

- Ask the children to describe their kitchens and identify its many uses. Ask them to plan the ideal kitchen for their family. What would they put in it? Using pictures from magazines and sales brochures, identify the various things one would find in a kitchen. 'Qu'est-ce que c'est?' 'C'est une machine à laver'. (What is this? It's a washing machine.) 'C'est la cuisinière.' (It's the cooker.)

- Discuss kitchen jobs in the family. 'Qui fait la lessive?' (Who does the washing?) 'Qui fait la cuisine?' (Who does the cooking?) 'Qui fait le repassage?' (Who does the ironing?) 'Qui débarrasse la table?' (Who clears the table?) and so on to elicit answers such as 'Ma soeur fait la lessive' (My sister does the washing.) 'Mon père fait la cuisine.' (My father does the cooking.) 'Ma mère fait le repassage.' (My mother does the ironing.) 'Je débarrasse la table.' (I clear the table.)

un bol

une tasse

une cuillère

une petite assiette

une grande assiette

une fourchette

un couteau

Further Activities

- Decorate different-sized paper plates, dishes and cups to create a tea/dinner service. Display and label them with the captions: 'une grande assiette' (a big plate), 'une petite assiette' (a small plate), 'une cuillère' (a spoon), 'une tasse' (a cup), 'un bol' (a bowl) and so on.

- In ICT, create simple lotto cards showing items that might be found in the kitchen cupboard and ask the question 'Qu'est-ce qu'il y a dans le placard?' (What's in the kitchen cupboard?) Replies could be 'une assiette' (a plate), 'un bol' (a bowl), 'une tasse', (a cup), 'une soucoupe' (a saucer) and so on.

- Gather together all the ingredients and utensils necessary to bake some biscuits. 'Voici la farine.' (Here is the flour.) 'Voici la balance.' (Here are the weighing scales.) 'Pèse la farine.' (Weigh the flour.) 'Mets la farine dans le bol.' (Put the flour in the bowl.) and so on, matching the simple sentences to the actions.

Conversation Model

- 'Tu manges les repas dans la cuisine?' (Do you eat your meals in the kitchen?)

- 'Oui.' (Yes.)

- 'Qui met la table?' (Who sets the table?)

- 'Je mets la table.' (I set the table.)

- 'Qui prépare le repas?' (Who gets the meal ready?)

- 'Ma mère prépare le repas.' (My mother gets the meal ready.)

- 'Qui fait la vaisselle?' (Who does the washing-up?)

- 'Le lave-vaisselle!' (The dishwasher!)

Making the Display

- Make a kitchen cupboard with opening doors from a cardboard carton. Put in a shelf that will support plastic plates and bowls and light kitchen utensils. Make a large sign saying 'Qu'est-ce qu'il y a dans le placard?' (What's in the kitchen cupboard?)

- Mount the cupboard, with the sign below it, centrally on the display board. Each day, put something different in the cupboard and let the children guess what is inside.

- Use cardboard cartons, fabric and other collage materials to make large models of kitchen appliances. Staple these to the display board with appropriate captions.

- Paint pictures of household items, cut out and add to the display with labels.

Vocabulary

la boîte à ordures (waste bin)
le bol (bowl)
la bouilloire (kettle)
les carreaux (tiles)
la casserole (saucepan)
le congélateur (freezer)
l'évier (sink)
le fer à repasser (iron)

le frigidaire/le frigo (fridge)
le grille-pain (toaster)
le lave-vaisselle (dishwasher)
le placard (cupboard)
la poêle (frying pan)
le séchoir à tambour (tumble dryer)
le tiroir (drawer)

Happy Christmas! (Joyeux Nöel!)

Starting Points

- Explain that in France certain Christmas customs are different to those in the UK. On 'la Veille de Nöel' (Christmas Eve) most people go to midnight Mass. The children put their shoes (not stockings) near the fireplace or Christmas tree for le Père Nöel (Father Christmas) to fill. After church, everyone sits down for the traditional Christmas meal or 'réveillon'. The children open their presents on Christmas morning. Everyone returns to work the next day.

- Talk about la Fête de Saint Sylvestre (the Feast of Saint Sylvestre), and 'la Veille du Nouvel An' (New Year's Eve). At midnight, French motorists sound their horns. 'Le Jour de l'An' (New Year's Day) is a time for visiting family and friends. More cards are sent in the New Year and early January than at Christmas.

- Talk about 'la Fête des Rois' (the Feast of the Kings) on 6 January. Epiphany is when the Wise Men came to worship Jesus. A celebratory meal is eaten in the evening and a special cake is shared between the guests. The cake is called La galette des Rois (cake of the kings) and contains 'une fève' (a small china ornament or charm). The person who receives this is crowned king of the feast.

Further Activities

- Make 'les papillotes à pétard' (Christmas crackers) from card tubes and crêpe paper and 'les guirlandes' (garlands or paper chains) from gummed paper.

- Make clay nativity figurines ('les santons'). Cut a quadrant shape from rolled-out clay, join the straight edges to form a cone and use this for the base of the figurine. Add head, headdress, cloak or crown according to the particular character. Explain how most French families have a set of nativity figurines and daily throughout Advent they are moved nearer to the crib, finally arriving on Christmas Eve.

- Recycle old Christmas cards to make New Year cards, using the phrases 'Meilleurs Voeux' (best wishes), 'Bonne Année' and 'Bonne et Heureuse Année' (Happy New Year). Explain that it is the custom in France to send cards for the first day of January.

Conversation Model

- 'Joyeux Noël, Christine!' (Merry Christmas, Christine.)

- 'Heureux Noël, Martin!' (Happy Christmas, Martin.)

- 'Tu as décoré le sapin de Noël?' (Have you decorated the Christmas tree?)

- 'Oui. Ma mère et moi nous avons décoré l'arbre de Noël aujourd'hui.' (Yes. My mother and I decorated the Christmas tree today.)

- 'Nous avons beaucoup de décorations.' (We have lots of decorations.)

- 'Nous avons beaucoup de décorations aussi et beaucoup de cadeaux.' (We have lots of decorations as well and lots of presents.)

Vocabulary

l'arbre/le sapin de Noël (Christmas tree)
la bûche de Noël (chocolate log)
les cadeaux (presents)
la crèche (crib/crib scene)
les décorations (decorations)
la dinde (turkey)
le foie gras (liver paté)
la guirlande (garland/trimming)
les huîtres (oysters)
le Jour de Noël (Christmas Day)
la Messe de Minuit (midnight Mass)
l'oie (goose)
le Père Noël (Father Christmas)
le réveillon (traditional meal eaten after midnight Mass)
le sabot de Noël (Christmas shoe)
les santons (nativity figurines)
le sapin (fir tree)
la Veille de Noël (Christmas Eve)

Making the Display

- Paint a snowy backdrop for the display area.

- Paint a large picture of Father Christmas and cut it out or use a large poster if you have one. Stand him at the back of the display area.

- Place small decorated Christmas trees around the cut-out Santa. Festoon with 'les décorations'.

- Wrap up boxes to look like Christmas presents. Print your own wrapping paper if possible. Arrange the presents (les cadeaux) around the trees and add labels.

The Feast of St Nicholas (La Fête de Saint Nicolas)

La Fête de Saint Nicolas

les maisons

la braderie

le sapin

l'étalage

l'arbre de Noël

Saint Nicolas

l'évêque

les enfants

la rue

Starting Points

- In northern and north-eastern France Christmas celebrations start on 6 December with 'la Fête de St Nicolas'. Talk about St Nicolas, the patron saint of children. He was a bishop who spent his life helping the poor, particularly children. He often went out at night disguised in a hooded cloak and left food, clothing or money at the doors of poor families. He died on the 6 December about 343CE.

- Talk about how the French celebrate 'la Fête de St Nicolas'. Children finish school early on 5 December and in the evening they leave shoes, containing letters saying what presents they would like for Christmas, by the fire ('la cheminée') for St Nicolas to read. The next morning they find their shoes filled with sweets, fruits and nuts. They also leave a carrot and a lump of sugar for St Nicolas' donkey. On the Sunday nearest to 6 December there is usually a street market ('braderie') in the town and a man dressed as a bishop walks along the streets giving sweets to the children.

la lettre

les sabots de Noël

Further Activities

- Write letters to St Nicolas. Paint pictures of shoes or 'les sabots de Noël' and cut out. Mount the shoes and letters on stiff card, arranging the letters to look as if they are placed in the shoes, then cut around them.

- Design and make 3-D sabots from stiff, coloured paper or felt. Use a slipper for the basic shape. Decorate with sequins and embroidery.

- Make simple sweets such as coconut ice, fudge, peppermint creams or chocolate shapes. Fill the sabots with sweets to take home as a Christmas gift.

⚠ **Food allergies!**

- Create a market stall in a corner of the classroom and display Christmas gifts, decorations and the children's sabots. Use the market stall to practise buying and selling in French.

Conversation Model

- 'Bonjour, Natalie!' (Hello, Natalie.)

- 'Bonjour, Simone. As-tu écrit une lettre à St Nicolas?' (Hello, Simone. Have you written a letter to St Nicholas?)

- 'Oui, j'ai écrit une lettre.' (Yes, I've written a letter.)

- 'Qu'est-ce que tu as demandé?' (What have you asked for?)

- 'J'ai demandé des livres et des CDs. Qu'est-ce que tu as demandé?' (I asked for some books and some CDs. What have you asked for?)

- 'J'ai demandé des jeux et une montre.' (I asked for some games and a watch.)

Making the Display

- Draw pictures of medieval French houses using black and brown wax crayons on grey or fawn paper. Cut out. Position these towards the top of the display board to form a town.

- Create market stalls using collage materials. Arrange these below the houses to form a street market.

- Use fabrics and wools to make people for the scene.

- Make a textured Christmas tree by covering a basic shape with cut and curled paper or fringed crêpe paper.

- Make a collage of St Nicolas using coloured paper or fabric and add to the display. Surround the figure with collaged children. Add labels.

Vocabulary

les bonbons (sweets)
la braderie (street market)
les cadeaux (presents)
la cheminée (the chimney or fireplace/hearth)
les décorations (decorations)
demander (to ask for)
écrire (to write)
l'étalage(m) (market stall)
l'évêque(m) (bishop)
les fruits (fruit)
une lettre (a letter)
la maison (house)
les noix (nuts)
la rue (street)
le sabot de Noël (Christmas shoe)
les souliers (shoes)

My Birthday (Mon Anniversaire)

Starting Points

- Ask the children their age: 'Quel âge as-tu?' (How old are you?), to which they answer 'J'ai dix ans.' (I'm ten.) and so on.

- Cut out pictures of babies, toddlers, children and teenagers from magazines and catalogues and mount them on card. Ask how old they think the various children are: 'Quel àge a-t-il/elle?' 'Il/elle a neuf mois/deux ans.' (What age is he/she? He/she is nine months/two years.) and so on.

- Ask the children when their birthdays are: 'C'est ton anniversaire quand?' (When is your birthday?), to which they reply 'C'est le douze mai.' (It's the twelfth of May.) and so on.

Further Activities

- Make birthday cards for different ages saying 'Bon anniversaire'. Take turns to hold up the cards saying who they are for, for example, 'Cette une carte pour Paul. Quel âge a-t-il?' Someone replies 'Il a six ans.' and so on.

- Ask each child to write out his or her name in large, brightly coloured letters and practise saying the letters in French.

- Hand print or use the computer to design wrapping paper and wrap up pretend presents to give to one another saying, 'Bon anniversaire, voici un cadeau.' (Happy Birthday, here's a present.)

- Make a model birthday cake so that different numbers of candles can be added. Use this to practise asking ages and so on. Other model party food could be made from salt dough and painted. Foam could be used to create sandwiches. Use paint and PVA for fillings.

- Bake a real birthday cake. Ask how many grams of the various ingredients are needed: 'Combien de grammes du sucre?' (How many grams of sugar?) and so on. Display and label the ingredients in French.

⚠ **Food allergies!**

Conversation Model

- 'Salut, Jacques.' (Hello, Jacques.)

- 'Salut, Kate. C'est ton anniversaire aujourd'hui, n'est-ce pas?' (Hello, Kate. It's your birthday today, isn't it?)

- 'Oui. J'ai onze ans.' (Yes. I'm eleven.)

- 'Tu as des cartes d'anniversaire?' (Have you got some birthday cards?)

- 'Oui, beaucoup!' (Yes, lots!)

- 'Combien?' (How many?)

- 'J'ai vingt cartes.' (I've got twenty cards.)

Making the Display

- Make A5 illuminated letters to spell out 'Bon anniversaire' and attach to the display board. The name of someone who is having a birthday soon can be added and changed as other birthdays happen.

- Decorate the board with balloons and streamers and the birthday cards made by the children.

- Place a table in front of the board and set as for a party with coloured plates, cups, paper serviettes, party hats (the children could make these) and the model birthday cake. Add French labels.

Vocabulary

le ballon (balloon)
la bougie (candle)
le cadeau (present)
la carte d'anniversaire (birthday card)
la fête d'anniversaire (birthday party)
le gâteau d'anniversaire (birthday cake)
le jeu (game)
le jouet (toy, plaything)

Going on Holiday (Aller en Vacances)

Starting Points

- Ask the children to describe holidays that they have had, how they got to their destination and what they did when they were there. Compile a list of methods of transport and show pictures of each. Describe the method of transport. 'Je suis allé(e) en voiture.' (I went by car.) 'Je suis allé(e) en avion/en bateau/en ferrie/en train/en car/en taxi/en bus/en vélo/en metro.' (I went by plane/boat/ferry/train/coach/taxi/bus/bike/the underground.)

- Ask where the children are going for their holidays this year: 'Où allez-vous passer les vacances cette année?' Introduce the expression 'Je vais aller …' (I am going to go …) and the reply, for example, 'Je vais aller en Espagne.' (I'm going to go to Spain.)

- Extend the sentences to include the mode of transport: 'Je vais aller en France en ferrie.' (I am going to go to France by ferry.) Then the length of stay: 'Je vais aller en France en ferrie pour dix jours.' (… for ten days.) Finally, add the month: 'Je vais aller en France en ferrie pour dix jours en juillet.' (… in July.)

C'est le costume national de quel pays?

Further Activities

- On a large-scale map of Europe, ask the children to find and mark the countries they have visited, saying as they do, for example, 'Je suis allée en Écosse.' (I went to Scotand.)

- Research the national costumes of various countries/regions. Make fabric collages or peg doll models. Ask 'C'est le costume national de quel pays?' 'C'est la costume de la Grèce.' (This is the national costume of which country? It's the costume of Greece.)

- In ICT, design posters advertising holidays in different countries, for example, 'Bienvenue en Angleterre'. Set up a travel agent's office ('l'agence de voyages') in a corner of the classroom and advertise '4 nuits à Paris en avril' (4 nights in Paris in April), '10 jours à Londres en août' (10 days in London in August) and so on.

- Paint the national flags of each country to hang around the classroom. Ask the question, for example, 'Cest le drapeau de quel pays?' (It's the flag of which country?) 'C'est le drapeau de la France.' (It's the flag of France.)

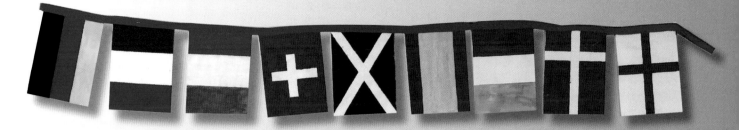

Making the Display

- Paint posters to represent each holiday destination, perhaps the Eiffel Tower for Paris, the Coliseum for Rome, a flamenco dancer for Spain. Place them on the display board interspersed with some of the ICT posters.

- Paint pictures of the various modes of transport. Cut out and mount between the posters. Add the appropriate label to each mode of transport.

- Finish the display with notices advertising offers from the travel agency.

Conversation Model

- 'Bonjour, Paul.' (Hello, Paul.)

- 'Bonjour, Christophe. Où as-tu passé tes vacances?' (Hello, Christopher. Where did you go for your holiday?)

- 'Je suis allé en Espagne.' (I went to Spain.)

- 'Pour combien de temps?' (How long for?)

- 'Pour deux semaines en juillet. Et toi?' (For two weeks in July. And you?)

- 'Je vais aller au Portugal pour dix jours en septembre.' (I'm going to Portugal for ten days in September.)

Vocabulary

Je vais aller en Allemagne (to Germany)
en Angleterre (to England)
en Belgique (to Belgium)
au Canada (to Canada)
au Danemark (to Denmark)
en Écosse (to Scotland)
en Grèce (to Greece)
en Irlande (to Ireland)
en Italie (to Italy)
en Norvège (to Norway)
au Pays de Galles (to Wales)
au Portugal (to Portugal)
en Suède (to Sweden)
en Suisse (to Switzerland)

A French-Speaking Country – Tunisia (Un Pays Francophone – La Tunisie)

Starting Points

- This topic can be used to revise work on travel, getting to know you and eating out. Identify French-speaking countries on a map of Europe. 'As-tu visité la France/la Suisse/la Belgique?' (Have you visited France/Switzerland/Belgium?) Encourage the children to say how they travelled: 'Je suis allé en Suisse en avion.' (I went to Switzerland by plane.)

- Identify French-speaking countries on a world map. 'As tu visité le Canada/le Maroc/l'Algérie/la Tunisie/la Martinique?' (Have you visited Canada/Morocco/Algeria/Tunisia/Martinique?) Some children may have relatives living in French-speaking countries or have had holidays at some of the popular tourist destinations where French is spoken. Invite them to share their experiences with the class.

- Choose a country that has particular relevance to the class. Show pictures of that country which illustrate its way of life. The children could do further research in the library and on the Internet. Compare life in that country with life at home.

Further Activities

- Paint Tunisian landscapes and Saharan sunsets and use to generate conversations. 'Qu'est-ce que c'est?' (What is it?) 'C'est la plage à Skanes. Voici les palmiers, le sable et la mer. Voici les touristes.' (It's the beach at Skanes. Here are the palm trees, the sand and the sea. Here are the tourists.)

- Use fabric and paint to create pictures of people wearing typical Arab dress. Ask 'Qu'est-ce qu'il/elle porte?' 'De quelle couleur est-ce?' and so on. (What is he/she wearing? What colour is it?)

- Look at recipes for typical Tunisian food. Compile a list in French of the spices used frequently in Tunisian cooking: l'anis (aniseed), la coriandre (coriander), le cumin (cumin), les graines de carvi (caraway seeds), la canelle (cinnamon), le safran (saffron).

- Prepare at home, or, if there is sufficient adult supervision, help the class to prepare a typical dish such as Tunisian carrot salad. List the instructions in simple French: éplucher (to peel), couper (to cut), cuire (to cook), égouter (to drain), ajouter (to add).

⚠ **Food allergies!**

Conversation Model

- 'Où vas-tu cet été?' (Where are you going this summer?)

- 'Je vais aller en Tunisie'. (I'm going to go to Tunisia.)

- 'Tu pars de quel aéroport?' (Which airport are you leaving from?)

- 'Birmingham.'

- 'Combien de temps prend-t-il?' (How long does it take?)

- 'Il prend deux heures et demie.' (It takes two and a half hours.)

Making the Display

- Draw a large camel on carton card. Cover the shape with screwed-up newspaper and then paste with layers of tissue or newsprint. Paint when dry. Position centrally on the display board.

- Paint Tunisian flags and arrange either side of the camel.

- Create postcards, travel brochures and posters and position on the display.

- Make a cardboard model of the El Jem Coliseum.

- Add a colourful border and labels.

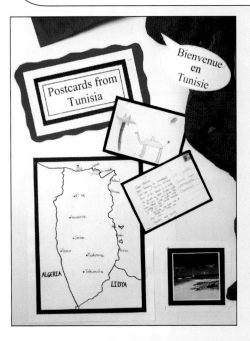

Vocabulary

l'aéroport (airport)	les passagers (the passengers)
l'agneau (lamb)	le passeport (passport)
les bagages (luggage)	la piste (the runway)
le chameau (camel)	le poisson (fish)
débarquer (to land)	la porte numéro 3 (gate
décoller (to take off)	number 3)
le désert (desert)	le puits de petrol (oil well)
la dune (sand dune)	le sable (sand)
la grande ville (city)	le serpent (snake)
le lizard (lizard)	le vol (the flight)
le palmier (palm tree)	

At the Campsite (Au Terrain de Camping)

Starting Points

- Ask if any of the children have been camping. If so, encourage them to share their experiences. These might range from camping in a small tent in a field with few facilities to staying on a site with restaurants and swimming pools.

- Show the children picture cards (or, even better, use actual camping equipment) and encourage them to guess the simple vocabulary: une tente (tent), une caravane (caravan), le sac de couchage (sleeping bag), un emplacement (a pitch), la réception (reception).

- Ask the children to bring in any photographs they have of camping holidays. Use these and pictures from brochures to ask, for example, 'Où est le terrain de camping?' (Where is the campsite?) 'Près de la rivière?' (Near the river?) 'Dans la campagne?' (In the country) 'Près de la plage?' (Near the beach?) 'Près d'un lac?' (Near a lake?)

Further Activities

- Paint and collage pictures of campsites using cut-outs from brochures. Stick on paper and paint a scene around them. Talk about the scenes. 'Où est la tente?' (Where is the tent?) 'La tente est à coté de la caravane.' (The tent is by the side of the caravan.) 'Où est le terrain de camping?' (Where is the campsite?) 'C'est dans la campagne à coté d'une forêt.' (It's in the countryside at the edge of a forest.)

- Allow each child to devise a set of small signs to represent the campsite facilities. They can use these in question and answer situations. 'Qu'est-ce que c'est?' (What is it?) 'C'est la salle de jeux?' (It's the games room.)

- Devise 'au camping' board games in the style of Ludo but with a tent or caravan at each corner of the board. Have forfeit and reward squares where the children have to pick up cards that send them to different markers on the board: 'Videz la poubelle.' (Empty the dustbin.) 'Allez au magasin.' (Go to the shop.) 'Faites la vaisselle.' (Do the dishes.)

Où est le terrain de camping?

Conversation Model

● 'Tu fais le camping?' (Do you go camping?)

● 'Oui. Toutes les vacances.' (Yes. Every holiday.)

● 'Où vas-tu?' (Where do you go?)

● 'Mes parents aiment aller à la campagne près d'un lac ou une rivière.' (My parents like to go to the countryside near a lake or a river.)

● 'Qu'est-ce qu'il y a au terrain de camping?' (What is there at the campsite?)

● 'Il y a un magasin, un restaurant, une salle de jeux et le tennis.' (There's a shop, a restaurant, a games room and tennis courts.)

Making the Display

● Paint a long strip of countryside background. Position along the top section of the display board.

● Cover the remainder of the display board with green paper or paint a background to represent grass.

● Paint pictures of different types of tent and caravan. Cut out and arrange on the field background.

● Create an entrance archway for the campsite.

● Paint signs to represent each of the facilities at the campsite. Mount these with labels underneath and arrange on the entrance framework and around the board.

● Add a green border to frame the display.

Vocabulary

un arbre (tree)
les bacs à vaisselle (pot washing area)
le bloc sanitaire (toilet block)
le champ (field)
une colline (hill)
un cours d'eau (stream)
l'emplacement (pitch)
jeux pour enfants (children's play area)
la laverie (laundry room)
les oiseaux (birds)
la piscine (swimming pool)
la poubelle (dustbin)
le restaurant (restaurant)
le sac de couchage (sleeping bag)
la salle de jeux (games room)

At the Seaside (Au Bord de la Mer)

le phare

la mouette

Au bord de la mer

la falaise

le bateau

un parasol

l'algue

le filet

le maillot de bain

le chateau de sable

les rochers

la plage

une pelle

la coquille

un seau

le transat

Starting Points

- Show the children pictures of beach scenes and people engaged in seaside activities. Make a class list of any vocabulary with which the children are already familiar.

- Talk about the pictures in simple sentences. 'Il joue dans le sable.' (He is playing in the sand.) 'Il a un seau et une pelle.' (He has a bucket and spade.) 'Il y a un bateau sur la mer.' (There is a boat on the sea.) When the children are familiar with the vocabulary, ask questions such as 'Qu'est-ce qu'il fait?' (What is he doing?) 'Quel temps fait-il?' (What is the weather like?)

Further Activities

- Look closely at the painting *At the Beach* by Edgar Degas and ask the children to describe the differences between that and a modern beach scene. Obtain a poster of the scene and cut this into sections. Give each child a section to copy, matching the original colours and brushstrokes as closely as possible. Ask 'Qu'est-ce que tu peins?' or 'Que peins-tu?' (What are you painting?) 'Je peins la mer/le ciel/le sable.' (I am painting the sea/the sky/the sand.) Revise colour vocabulary.

- Paint beach and coastal scenes. The children could describe their paintings. 'Il y a un phare sur la falaise.' (There is a lighthouse on the cliff.) 'Le petit garçon joue avec un ballon.' (The little boy is playing with a ball.)

- Reproduce the painting as a weaving (un tissage) and a fabric collage (un collage de tissue). Make a number of small card looms and weave panels of sky, sea and sand using a variety of shades and textures of wool. Sew these together or glue them onto a backing sheet. Create separate figures from material and glue these onto the weaving.

Conversation Model

- 'Où vas-tu passer les vacances cette année?' (Where are you going to spend your holidays this year?)

- 'À la côte sur un terrain de camping.' (At the coast on a campsite.)

- 'Qu'est-ce que tu aimes faire à la côte?' (What do you like doing at the coast?)

- 'J'aime nager dans la mer.' (I like swimming in the sea.)

- 'Moi, j'aime prendre un bain de soleil.' (I like to sunbathe.)

- 'J'aime grimper sur les rochers.' (I like to climb on the rocks.)

Making the Display

- Cover the top part of the display board with pale blue paper.

- Cut a strip of paper the width of the display board and use tissue paper, chiffon and net to create the sea. Similarly, use a variety of collage materials to create the beach. Mount these on the board.

- Use textured wallpaper for the cliffs and rocks.

- Paint or collage figures, boats, birds, buckets, spades and so on. Cut them out and add to the display.

- Add a colourful border and clear labels.

Vocabulary

l'algue (f) (seaweed)
l'âne (m) (donkey)
le bateau de pêche (fishing boat)
le caillou (pebble)
le château de sable (sandcastle)
la coquille (shell)
la côte (coast)
le crabe (crab)
la falaise (cliff)
le filet (net)
l'île (f) (island)

le maillot de bain (swimsuit)
la mer (sea)
la mer entre les rochers (rock pool)
la mouette (seagull)
les palmes (flippers)
le phare (lighthouse)
la plage (beach)
les rochers (rocks)
le seau (bucket)
le transat (deckchair)
la vague (wave)

55

The Farm (La Ferme)

La Ferme

la poule

le porcelet

le tracteur

l'oie

le canard

le fermier

le cochon

l'agneau

le mouton

la vache

le veau

Starting Points

- The children's experience of farms and farm life will be varied. Ask them to share any experiences they have had. If necessary, they can describe what they have seen on television or read in books. Ask them to draw pictures of what they would expect to find on a farm and to discuss. 'Qu'est-ce que c'est?' (What is this?) 'C'est un tracteur.' (It's a tracteur.) 'C'est une remorque.' (It's a trailer.) 'C'est le fermier.' (It's the farmer.)

- In simple terms, talk about the work the farmer does. 'Il travaille dans les champs.' (He works in the fields.) 'Au printemps il sème les graines.' (In spring he sows the seeds.) 'Il arrose les plantes.' (He waters the plants.) 'Il coupe le blé.' (He cuts the wheat).

- Set up a model farm. Encourage the children to look up the vocabulary for the various models in simple picture French dictionaries.

Further Activities

- Paint pictures of animal families and ask the children to describe what they have painted. 'Voici la poule. Voici le coq et voici les petits poussins.' (Here is the hen. Here is the cockerel and here are the little chicks.)

- Make sets of playing cards for the children to play 'Happy Families'. One set of cards could include pictures of le fermier (the farmer), la fermière (the farmer's wife), la ferme (the farm), le tracteur (the tractor), la remorque (the trailer), la paille (straw), le blé (wheat). Another set could be entirely of animals.

- Make 3-D papier mâché or clay models of the various farm animals. Ask the children what they are making. 'Je fais un taureau.' (I am making a bull.)

Conversation Model

- 'Où vas-tu passer les vacances cette année?' (Where are you going for your holiday this year?)

- 'Je vais rester sur une ferme.' (I'm going to stay on a farm.)

- 'Est-ce qu'il y des animaux?' (Are there any animals?)

- 'Oui. Il y a des vaches, des cochons et des poules.' (Yes. There are some cows, some pigs and some hens.)

- 'Est-ce qu'il y a de moutons?' (Are there any sheep?)

- 'Non. Il n'y a pas des moutons.' (No. There aren't any sheep.)

Making the Display

- Paint pictures of a tractor, sacks of corn, a barn, a pigsty and so on and cut them out.

- Draw farm animal shapes on carton card and cut out. Stick screwed-up newspaper to the card to build up the shape. Paste with layers of torn paper to make a smooth surface. Paint when dry.

- Arrange the cut-out paintings and the papier mâché shapes on the display board and label clearly.

Vocabulary

l'agneau (lamb)
le ballot de paille (straw bale)
la boue (mud)
le canard (duck)
le caneton (duckling)
les champs (fields)
le chien de berger (sheepdog)
le cochon (pig)
le coq (cockerel)
le dindon (turkey)
l'étable (cowshed)
la grange (barn)
l'hangar (large shed)
la mare (pond)
le mouton (sheep)
l'oie(f) (goose)
l'oison (gosling)
le porcelet (piglet)
la porcherie (pigsty)
le poulailler (henhouse)
la poule (hen)
le poussin (chick)
le sac de blé (sack of wheat)
le taureau (bull)
la vache (cow)
le veau (calf)

In the Town (À la Ville)

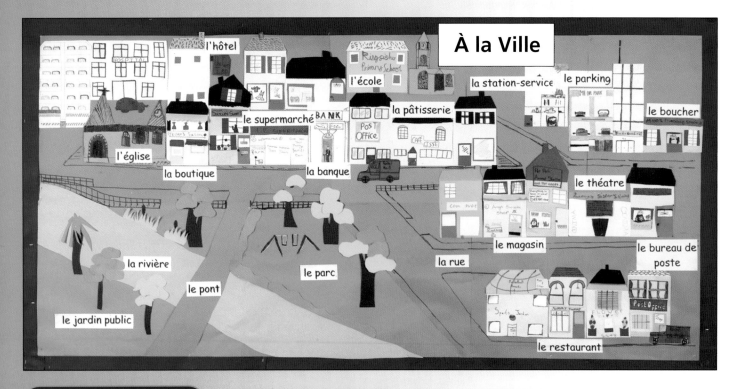

Starting Points

- Ask the children to name the different kinds of buildings that they have seen in the local town, such as the bank, post office, shops, museum and so on. Take photographs of these buildings to use as flashcards to ask questions. 'Qu'est-ce que c'est?' (What is it?) 'C'est une banque.' (It's a bank.) 'C'est la gare.' (It's the station.) 'C'est un café.' (It's a café.)

- Introduce phrases for asking and giving directions. 'Où est la gare?'/'Où se trouve la gare?' (Where is the station?) 'Je cherche une banque.' (I'm looking for a bank.) 'Il y a une banque près d'ici, s'il vous plaît?' (Is there a bank near here, please?)

Further Activities

- Draw or paint A3-sized street plans showing the key buildings of the town. Use these to practise the vocabulary for asking and giving directions. 'Où sont les magasins, s'il vous plaît?' (Where are the shops, please?) 'Traversez la rue/place.' (Cross the road/square.) 'Montez/descendez la rue.' (Go up/go down the street.) 'Prenez la deuxième rue à gauche.' (Take the second street on the left.)

- Draw a straight street with buildings and shops on both sides of the street. Practise phrases such as 'La poste est en face de la boulangerie.' (The post office is opposite the bakers.) 'La patisserie est à côté du boucherie.' (The cake shop is next to the butcher.) 'La banque est au bout de la rue.' (The bank is at the end of the street.)

- Make small cardboard boxes into buildings such as le bureau de poste (post office), la boucherie (butcher's), la banque (bank), la boutique (boutique), le supermarché (supermarket) and so on, and group to form a town centre. Use the model to practise asking directions.

Conversation Model

- 'Bonjour. Excusez moi, je cherche le syndicat d'initiative.' (Hello. Excuse me, I'm looking for the tourist information office.)
- 'Allez tout droit.' (Go straight on.)
- 'Oui.' (Yes.)
- 'Et puis prenez la première rue à droite.' (And then take the first street on the right.)
- 'Merci beaucoup.' (Thank you very much.)
- 'C'est à gauche!' (It's on the left.)
- 'Merci! Au revoir.' (Thanks! Goodbye.)

Making the Display

- Paint or make A4 paper collages of all the main buildings in the town and cut them out.
- Cover the display board with light grey paper and on this mark out a street plan, adding a river and a bridge.
- Arrange the buildings along the streets to create a plan of the town.
- Add the vocabulary for the buildings and key phrases.
- Use the display as part of the lesson, asking questions such as: 'Où est ton bâtiment?' (Where is your building?) 'C'est à côté du restaurant.' (It's next to the restaurant.) 'Qu'est-ce que c'est?' (What is it?) 'C'est une boulangerie.' (It's a bakery.)

Vocabulary

la boucherie (butcher's)
la boulangerie (bakery)
le bureau de poste (post office)
le cinéma (cinema)
le college (college)
le commissariat de police (police station)
l'église (church)
l'hôtel (hotel)
l'hôtel de ville (town hall)
le jardin public/le parc (park)
le magasin (shop)
le musée (museum)
le parking (parking/car park)
le pont (bridge)
la rivière (river)
la station-service (filling station)
le syndicat d'initiative (tourist information)
le théâtre (theatre)

Transport (Le Transport)

Starting Points

- Ask the children how they get to school. Most probably arrive by foot (à pied) or by car (en voiture). Some may arrive by bus (en bus) or on a bicycle (à vélo). Ask how other members of the family travel to work or to secondary school.

- Draw a graph to show the results of the survey and discuss. 'Je vais à l'école à pied.' (I go to school on foot.) or 'Douze enfants vont à l'école à pied.' (Twelve children go to school on foot.) 'Trois enfants vont à l'école à vélo.' (Three children go to school by bike.)

- Talk about holidays and how the children get there. 'Je vais à Londres en train.' (I am going to London by train). 'Je vais à Paris en avion.' (I am going to Paris by plane.) 'Je vais en France en bateau.' (I am going to France by boat.)

Further Activities

- Draw, paint or collage large pictures of vehicles and label the various parts, such as une roue (wheel), un pneu (tyre), le volant (steering wheel), les phares (headlights), une vitre (window), la ceinture de sécurité (seatbelt), le coffre (the boot) and so on.

- In ICT, ask the children to make sets of cards, each card showing a different vehicle. Use these to play 'Happy Families' in small groups, each child taking it in turn to ask 'As-tu un camion/une voiture/un vélo?' (Have you got a lorry/car/bike?) and so on.

- Give the children sheets of large-squared graph paper and ask them to draw a different vehicle in each square. Use these sheets to play 'Lotto'. When a child shouts 'Lotto! J'ai gagné!' (Bingo! I've won!), ask what vehicles he/she has covered/ marked on the sheet.

- In Design and Technology, make moving models of vehicles from packaging, dowel, cotton reels and card discs and name the parts in French.

Conversation Model

- 'Je vais à l'école à pied. Qu'est-ce tu fait?' (I go to school on foot. What do you do?)

- 'Je vais en voiture avec ma mère.' (I go by car with my mother.)

- 'Mon père va au travail en voiture.' (My father goes to work by car.)

- 'Mon père va au travail en train.' (My father goes to work by train.)

- 'Nous allons à Londres en train.' (We go to London by train.)

- 'Nous allons en car.' (We go by coach.)

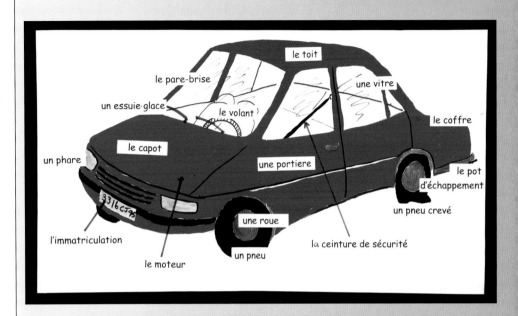

Making the Display

- Draw and cut out vehicles from coloured papers. Cut out the windows and glue white or silver paper behind the holes and draw the passengers and so on. Add detail to bodywork in felt-tipped pen.

- Collage A4-sized shop fronts and High Street buildings using a range of coloured papers. Add detail in felt-tipped pen.

- Assemble the buildings on a light blue and grey background to resemble a high street, tucking some buildings behind others to give depth to the picture.

Vocabulary

une ambulance (ambulance)
un autobus (bus)
un avion (aeroplane)
un bateau (boat)
un camion (lorry)
une camionette (van)
un car (coach)
la circulation (traffic)
un embouteillage (traffic jam)
un fourgon (van)
une moto (motorbike)
un taxi (taxi)
un train (train)
les vehicules (vehicles)
un vélo (bicycle)
une voiture (car)
une voiture de police (police car)

- Add the vehicles to create a busy road. Add a viaduct if necessary to accommodate a train or canal boat.

- If desired, collage and cut out figures and add to the scene. Add labels and a border.

At the Post Office (À la Poste)

Starting Points

- Ask the class about their local post office. Can they name the services provided by the post office? Do they know that the postboxes in France are a different colour (yellow) to the ones in Great Britain?

- Show them articles that can be bought/seen at a post office. 'Qu'est-ce que c'est?' (What is it?) 'C'est un timbre.' (It's a postage stamp.) 'C'est une enveloppe.' ('It's an envelope.') 'C'est une carte postale.' (It's a postcard.) Practise asking for various items.

Further Activities

- Make a boîte à lettres (postbox) from a cardboard box covered in yellow paper. Provide envelopes and paper. Write correctly addressed letters to children and staff. Elect a new 'facteur' (postman) each day to sort and deliver 'le courrier' (the mail), using phrases such as 'Voici une letter pour toi/vous.' (Here is a letter for you.) 'Tu as deux cartes postales.' (You have two postcards.)

- Set up a counter, labelled 'le guichet', in a corner of the classroom where the children can play and practise simple phrases such as 'Deux timbres, s'il vous plaît'.

- Design, colour and write postcards to take to 'La Poste'.

- Design and paint special commemorative stamps.

- Design sheets of stamps in ICT.

Conversation Model

- 'Bonjour. Je voudrais envoyer une lettre en Angleterre, s'il vous plaît.' (Good morning. I'd like to send a letter to England please.)

- 'Cinquante cents, s'il vous plaît.' (Fifty cents, please.)

- 'Donnez-moi trois cartes postales et trois timbres aussi.' (Give me three postcards and three stamps as well.)

- 'Voilà. Ça fait trois euros cinquante.' (There you are. That's three euros fifty.)

- 'Merci. Où est la boîte à lettres?' (Thank you. Where is the postbox?)

- 'À gauche, près de la sortie.' (On the left, near the way out.)

Making the Display

- On A2 paper, draw and paint the head and shoulders of three 'employées' to put behind the counter. Cut out.

- Ask the children to draw around each other on lengths of wallpaper or lining paper to create life-sized customers. Paint and cut out.

- Cut 'un boîte à lettres' (postbox) from yellow paper and position on the display.

- Add 'une cabine téléphonique' (telephone box).

- Cut out speech bubbles with appropriate phrases and position by the figures.

- Add a display of postcards, birthday cards and other things found in the post office.

- Add signs above each 'guichet' indicating the service available, such as 'Vente de Timbres' (sale of stamps) and 'Renseignements' (information).

Vocabulary

l'adresse (address)
l'annuaire de telephone (telephone directory)
une boîte à lettres (postbox)
une cabine téléphonique (telephone box)
un colis (parcel)
le facteur (postman)
les fiches/les formulaires/les imprimés (forms)
le guichet (counter)
une lettre (letter)
un paquet (package)
par avion (airmail)
par retour du courier (by return of post)
un téléphone public (public telephone)

At the Restaurant (Au Restaurant)

Starting Points

- Ask the children where they like to go when they eat out. Make a list of favourite eating places. 'Qu'est-ce que tu aimes manger?' (What do you like to eat?)

- Hold up pictures of various foods and menus from local takeaways and ask questions such as 'Tu aimes la salade?' (Do you like salad?) 'Tu aimes la pizza?' (Do you like pizza?) Tu manges les frites?' (Do you eat chips?). Encourage responses, for example, 'Oui. J'aime la salade' or 'Non. Je n'aime pas la salade.'

- Ask 'Qu'est-ce que tu aimes boire?' (What do you like to drink?) Show pictures of various drinks and ask 'Tu aimes le thé/café/jus d'orange?' (Do you like tea/coffee/orange juice?)

Further Activities

- Draw and paint table settings showing the children's favourite meals. Use these to introduce the vocabulary for knife (un couteau), fork (une fourchette), spoon (une cuillère), plate (une assiette), drinking glass (un verre), tablecloth (une nappe) and napkin (une serviette).

- Use a selection of collage materials, such as card, art straws, sponge, wool, beads and coloured paper, to create representations of favourite meals. Ask the children to describe what they have made, for example, 'J'ai fait une salade et les tomates et les pommes de terres.' (I have made a salad and tomatoes and potatoes.)

- Set up a restaurant table in the corner of the classroom and encourage role-play using the conversation model and the collaged meals. Take turns playing the waiter and the customer.

- In ICT, design simple menu cards to use in the role-play.

- As part of a 'Healthy Eating' topic, make a block graph of favourite foods and drinks. Ask 'Combien d'enfants mangent les frites?' (How many children eat chips?). 'Combien préfèrent la salade?' (How many prefer salad?) and so on.

Conversation Model

- 'Bonjour, monsieur/madame.' (Hello, sir/madam.)

- 'Bonjour. Je voudrais un sandwich au jambon, s'il vous plaît.' (Hello. I would like a ham sandwich, please.)

- 'Et comme boisson?' (And to drink?)

- 'Un jus d'orange, s'il vous plaît.' (An orange juice, please.)

- 'C'est tout?' (Is that all?)

- 'Non. Je voudrais une glace.' (No. I would like an ice cream.)

- 'De quel parfum?' (What flavour?)

- 'Chocolat, s'il vous plaît.' (Chocolate, please.)

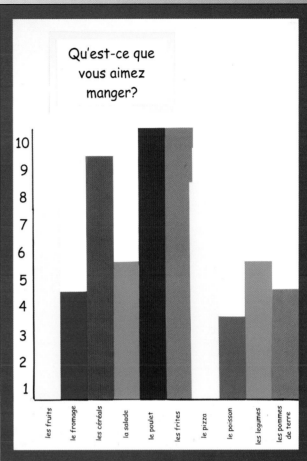

Making the Display

- Cut out a paper doorway and mount at one end of the display area.

- Arrange drapes at each side of the remaining space and tie back as curtains.

- Mount some of the simple menu cards and arrange in the 'window'.

- Paint and cut out the table and figures and arrange centrally on the display.

- Add large speech bubbles and labels.

Vocabulary

les boissons (drinks)
les carottes (carrots)
chocolat (chocolate)
citron (lemon)
l'eau minérale (mineral water)
la fraise (strawberry)
les frites (chips)
le fromage (cheese)
la glace (ice cream)
le hamburger (hamburger)
la limonade (lemonade)
les parfums (flavours)
les petits pois (peas)
le pizza (pizza)

les pommes de terre (potatoes)
le poulet (chicken)
la salade (salad)
un sandwich au fromage (a cheese sandwich)
un sandwich au jambon (a ham sandwich)
la saucisse (sausage)
les spaghetti
les tomates (tomatoes)
la viande (meat)
le yaourt (yogurt)

At the Supermarket (Au Supermarché)

Starting Points

- Ask the children to describe the local supermarkets and their products. Do all of their families shop at the same supermarket? Ask 'Qui aime aller au supermarché?' (Who likes to go to the supermarket?) 'Qui aime faire les courses?' (Who likes doing the shopping?) 'Où vas-tu?' (Where do you go?) Encourage responses such as 'J'aime faire les courses avec ma mere.' (I like to do the shopping with my mother.) 'Je n'aime pas aller au supermarché.' (I don't like going to the supermarket.) 'Je vais chez … [name of supermarket] (I go to …) or 'Je fais les courses à …' (I do the shopping at …)

- Talk about French supermarkets. Put up the names of French supermarkets, such as Champion, Leclerc, Intermarché, Casino and Géant, and play elimination games. The children move to the supermarket of their choice, a name is drawn from a hat and 'Tous les enfants qui font les courses à Champion sont éliminés!' (All the children who shop at Champion are out!)

Further Activities

- Design nets for packaging and new labels in French for existing boxes, packets and plastic bottles. (Please ensure the latter are well washed out.) Simply use the name of the product, for example le lait (milk), le beurre (butter), la limonade (lemonade), le fromage (cheese). Use these boxes, bottles and packets to set up a supermarket in the corner of the classroom where the children can shop and practise the vocabulary.

- Use collage materials and papier mâché to create models of fish, lobster, meat and chicken to add to the supermarket display.

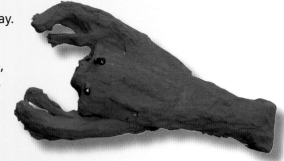

- Examine French currency and make replica coins and notes.

- Make shopping lists in French with prices in euros. For example, une baguette 0,70 euro, le lait 0,90 euro, le fromage 2,90 euro, les tomates 1,25 euro. Use the currency in the role-play area to practise addition and subtraction whilst buying the goods and receiving change.

- Design and make carrier bags for imaginary supermarket chains.

Conversation Model

- 'Tu fais les courses?' (Do you do the shopping?)

- 'Oui. Tous les jeudis soirs avec ma mère.' (Yes. Every Thursday evening with my mother.)

- 'Je n'aime pas faire les courses.' (I don't like shopping.)

- 'J'aime pousser le chariot.' (I like pushing the trolley.)

- 'Tu achètes beaucoup?' (Do you buy a lot?)

- 'Oui. J'achète beaucoup.' (Yes. I buy a lot.)

Making the Display

- Make a large figure for the shop assistant. Cut out and mount at one end of the display board.

- Make a till from carton card and fix to the display.

- Create a conveyor belt strong enough to support some of the packets, boxes and papier-maché foods that the children have created.

- Staple a row of boxes to the display to look like a shelf full of products.

- Create a basket from woven paper and strips of card.

- Add a colourful border and labels.

Vocabulary

l'argent (money)
la balance (weighing scales)
un bocal/les bocaux (jar/jars)
une boîte (a tin)
une boîte de saumon (tin of salmon)
une bouteille (a bottle)
la caisse (checkout)
le chariot (trolley)
le panier (basket)
un paquet (packet)
peser (to weigh)
le porte-monnaie (purse)
le sac à main (handbag)
les sac en plastiques (plastic bags)
le vendeur/la vendeuse (shop assistant)

At the Station (À la Gare)

Starting Points

- If possible, arrange a trip to the local railway station. Make a display of pictures illustrating the various areas and signs to be found in a station. Alternatively, take photographs of the local station and see if the children can identify them.

- Ask how many children have travelled from the local station. Ask them to describe their experiences. Show pictures or photographs of signs to be found around the station. Make sure that the children know what they are in English before practising the French words.

- Practise asking for single and return tickets to various towns. 'Un aller simple pour Manchester, s'il vous plaît.' (A single to Manchester, please.) 'Un aller-retour pour Londres, s'il vous plaît.' (A return ticket to London, please.) Ask which platform the train leaves from. 'Le train part de quel quai?' 'Le train part/arrive à quelle heure?' (What time does the train leave/arrive?)

Further Activities

- Design original signs for the different areas of the station, such as 'la salle d'attente' (the waiting room). Mount these with the appropriate caption underneath.

- Make smaller versions of these to use as playing cards in group games. Practise the vocabulary by playing 'Remembrance', naming each card as it is turned over.

- Invent timetables and use to practise phrases such as 'Le train pour Sheffield part à huit heures.' (The train for Sheffield leaves at eight o'clock.)

Conversation Model

- 'Bonjour, monsieur.' (Good morning, sir.)
- 'Bonjour. Vous désirez?' (Good morning. What would you like?)
- 'Un aller-retour pour Londres, s'il vous plaît.' (A return ticket to London, please.)
- 'Première ou deuxième classe?' (First or second class?)
- 'Deuxième, s'il vous plaît.' (Second class, please.)
- 'Voilà.' (Here you are.)
- 'Le train part de quel quai?' (Which platform does the train leave from?)
- 'Quai numéro 8.' (Platform number 8.)
- 'Merci, monsieur. Au revoir.' (Thank you, sir. Goodbye.)

Destinations	Départs	Quai	Arrivées
Doncaster	09.30	3	10.00
Londres	09.35	5	11.05
Newcastle	09.45	1	11.45
Birmingham	09.55	4	11.10
Plymouth	10.00	2	13.30
Oxford	10.15	4	12.00
Sheffield	25		11.15

Le train part de quel quai?

Le train arrive à quelle heure?

A quelle heure part le train pour Doncaster?

Making the Display

- The children create life-sized passengers by drawing around each other on lengths of lining or wallpaper. Paint and cut out. Ask for adult volunteers for the same purpose!
- Create a life-sized head and shoulders for the person in the ticket office. Mount this on a rectangle of yellow paper. Mount again to create a frame.
- Position the ticket office window on the board and arrange the passengers in a queue.
- Cut out speech bubbles and display the phrases the children have practised.
- Complete the display with a selection of station signs and add labels.

le buffet

Vocabulary

un aller-retour (return ticket)
un aller simple (single ticket)
le billet (ticket)
le buffet (restaurant)
le bureau des objets trouvés (lost property office)
le chariot (luggage trolley)
le composteur (ticket machine)
la consigne (left luggage)

entrée (entrance)
fumeur (smoking)
le guichet (ticket office)
non-fumeur (non-smoking)
le quai (platform)
les renseignements (information)
la salle d'attente (waiting room)
sortie (exit)
le train (train)

At the Market (Au Marché)

Labels on display: les oranges, Au Marché, les bananes, les pommes, les poireaux, les oignons, le chou-fleur, les carottes, les tomates

Starting Points

- Look at photographs and pictures of local and French markets and identify the range of produce. Use this activity to build up a vocabulary bank.

- Make a collection of plastic/imitation fruit and vegetables with corresponding labels. The children take it in turns to match the label to the correct fruit or vegetable. Use the phrases from the conversation model to practise buying and selling the produce.

Further Activities

- Make sets of playing cards featuring fruit and vegetables. Play 'Happy Families' or 'Five of a Kind', asking 'As-tu les raisins?' or 'As-tu les fraises?' and so on until a full set is collected. The negative form 'Non. Je n'ai pas les raisins/les fraises.' can be taught here. Play 'Snap' or 'Remembrance', saying the name of the fruit or vegetable as each card is turned over.

- Make still life compositions of fruit and vegetables for observational drawing and discuss them in French. 'Voici une pomme, deux bananes et une orange.' (Here is an apple, two bananas and an orange.) 'Dessinez les fruits!' (Draw the fruit.)

- Ask each child to make a textile representation of a fruit or vegetable on a natural hessian backing. Encourage them to say what they are making. 'Je fais un chou-fleur.' (I am making a cauliflower.) 'Je fais des raisins.' (I am making some grapes). Join the separate pieces into a large wall hanging. Use in the lesson to ask 'Qu'est-ce que c'est?/Qu'est-ce que ce sont?' (What is it?/What are they?)

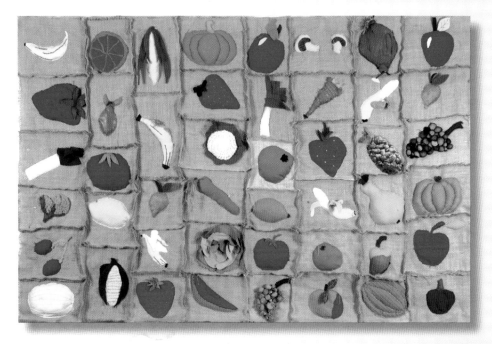

- Create a free-standing market stall on which to display fruit and vegetables. Secure lengths of timber to the four corners of a display table. Cut lengths of brightly coloured paper or card and secure to the tops of the lengths of timber to create the impression of a canopy.

- Cover the table in fake grass, green paper or cloth. If possible, furnish the stall with actual market/supermarket punnets, salad trays and boxes. Add a pair of scales and a cash register.

- Make papier-mâché fruit and vegetables by screwing up sheets of newspaper into ball-like shapes and covering with layers of pasted paper. Either use coloured papers or paint when the shape is dry. Create cabbages, cauliflowers and lettuce by cutting out leaf shapes from crêpe paper and gluing around a basic papier-mâché shape. Alternatively, use real fruit and vegetables.

- Make representations of euro notes and coins. Use the display for role-play in the classroom.

- Create a market stall holder from chicken wire and Modroc.

Conversation Model

- 'Bonjour. Qu'est-ce que vous désirez?' (Good morning. What would you like?)

- 'Bonjour. Je voudrais un kilo de pommes de terre, s'il vous plaît.' (Good morning. I would like a kilogram of potatoes, please.)

- 'Voilà. C'est tout?' (Here you are. Is that all?)

- 'Non. Je voudrais un chou-fleur et un melon, s'il vous plait.' (No. I would like a cauliflower and a melon, please.)

- 'Voilà.' (Here you are.)

- 'Merci. Ça fait combien?' (Thank you. How much is that?)

- 'Ça fait cinq euros, s'il vous plaît.' (That's five euros, please.)

- 'Merci. Au revoir.' (Thank you. Goodbye.)

Vocabulary

l'abricot (apricot)
l'ananas (pineapple)
la banane (banana)
la carotte (carrot)
la cerise (cherry)
le champignon (mushroom)
le citron (lemon)
le chou (cabbage)
le chou-fleur (cauliflower)

les choux de Bruxelles (sprouts)
la fraise (strawberry)
la framboise (raspberry)
les fruits (fruit)
les haricots verts (green beans)
la laitue (lettuce)
les légumes (vegetables)
le melon (melon)
l'oignon (onion)

l'orange (orange)
le pamplemousse (grapefruit)
la pêche (peach)
la poire (pear)
le poireau (leek)
les pois (peas)
la pomme (apple)
la pomme de terre (potato)
les raisins (grapes)
la tomate (tomato)

J'aime faire le jardinage.

l'arbre

Dans le jardin

l'abri jardin

le jet d'eau

la bêche

la fleur

les feuilles

In the Garden (Dans le Jardin) (page 36)